This Coloring Book Is Dedicated To

My Son Rashad and his brother Tiqi and his sister Nevaeh.

I can’t do anything but love you.

~ Artist Nicholas Showers-Glover

Let The Color Motivate You

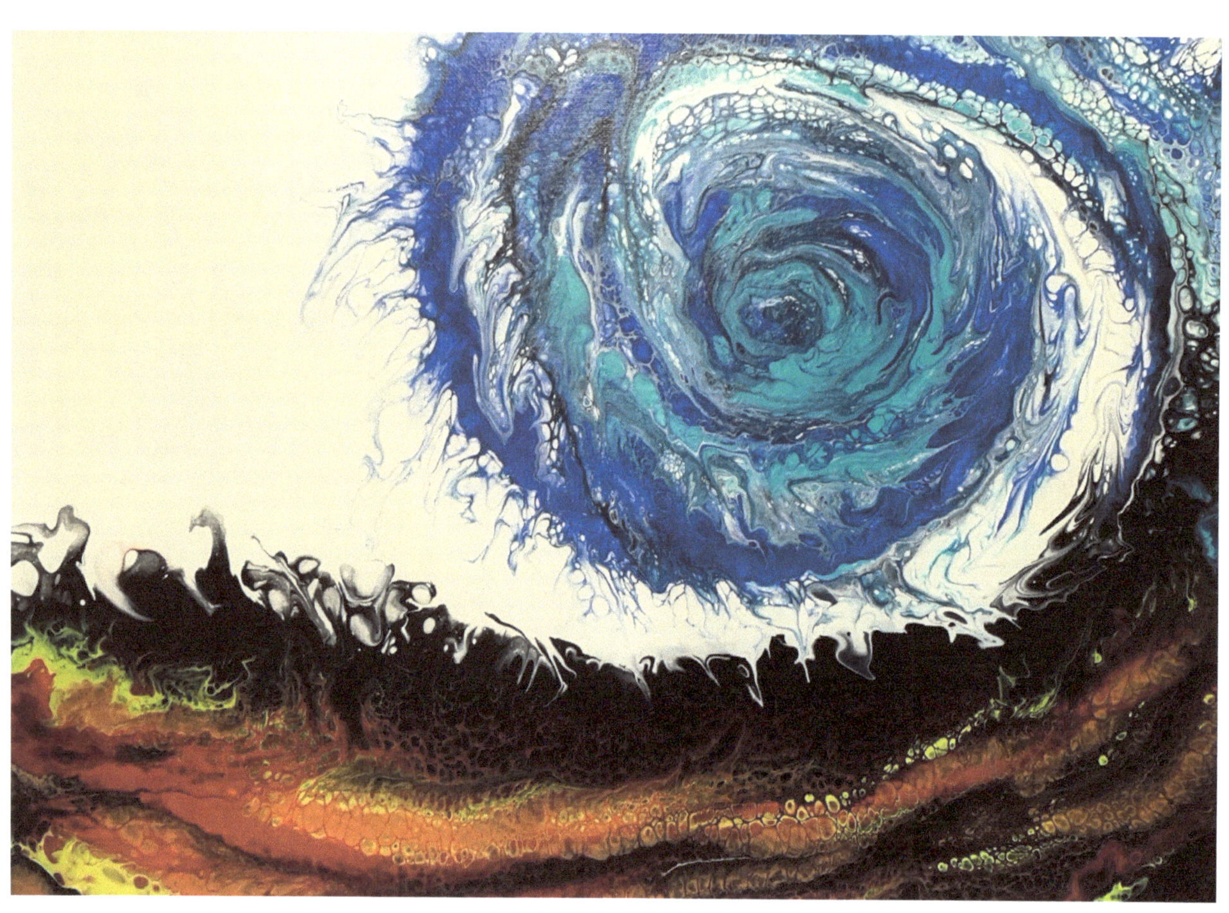

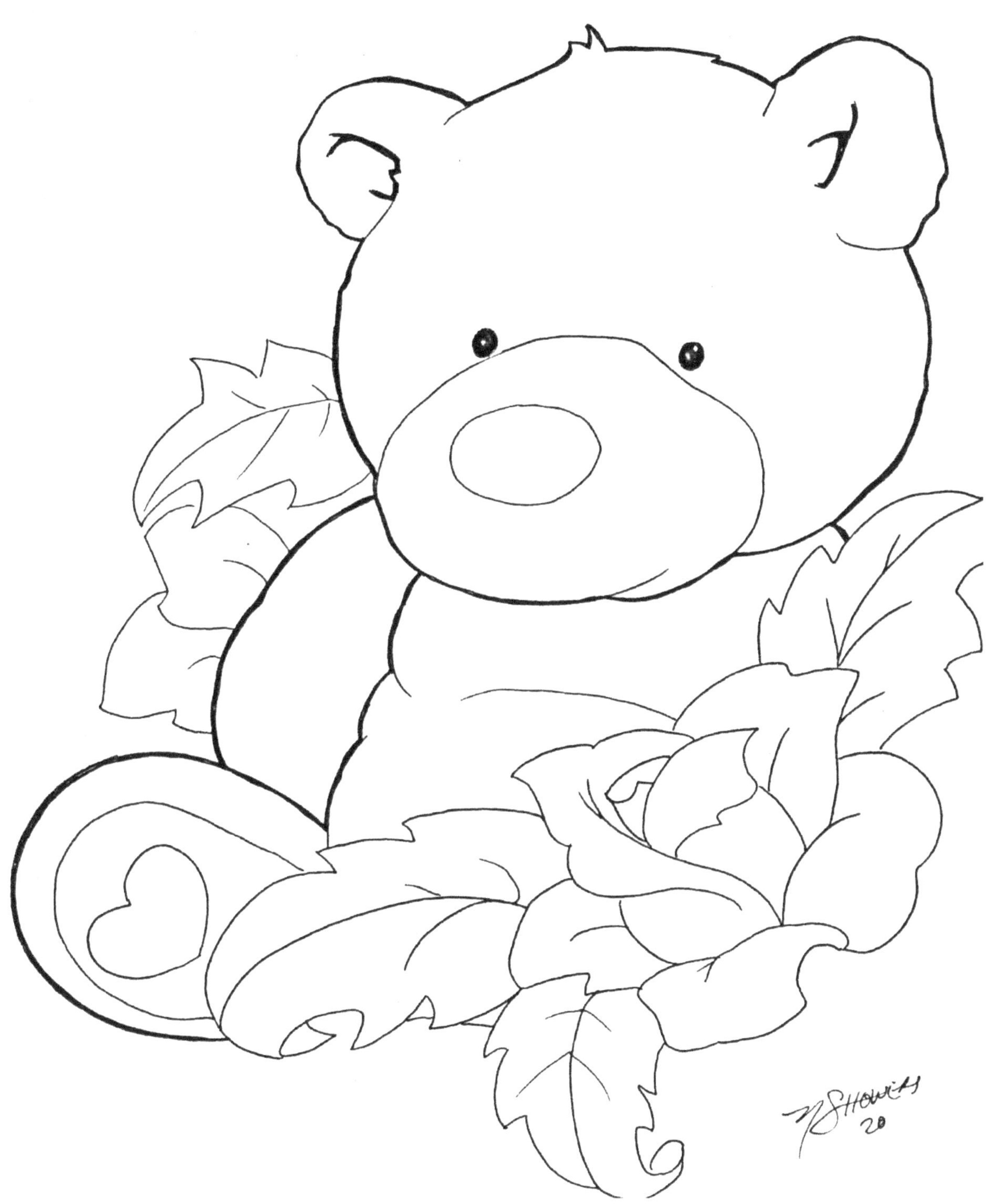

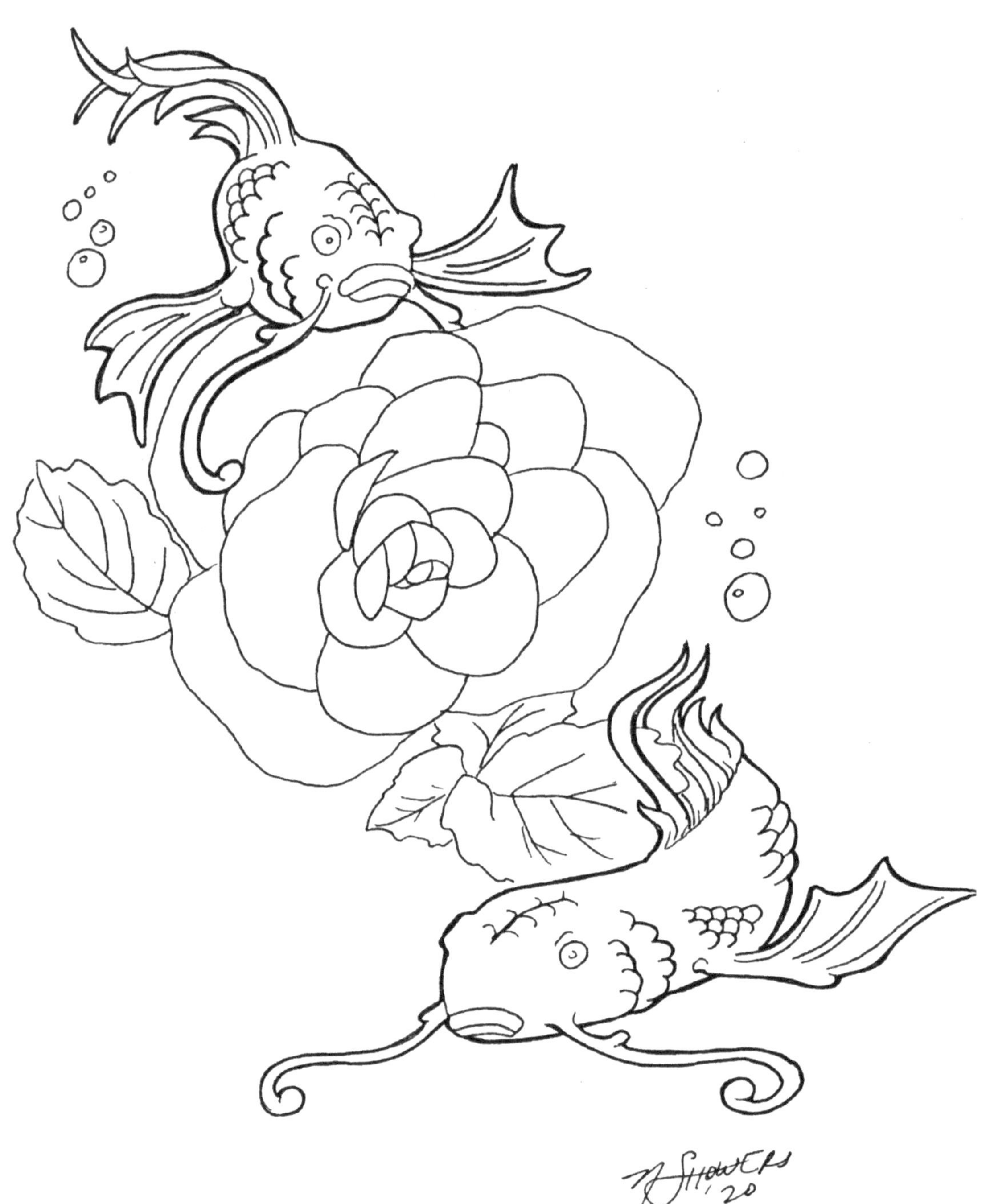

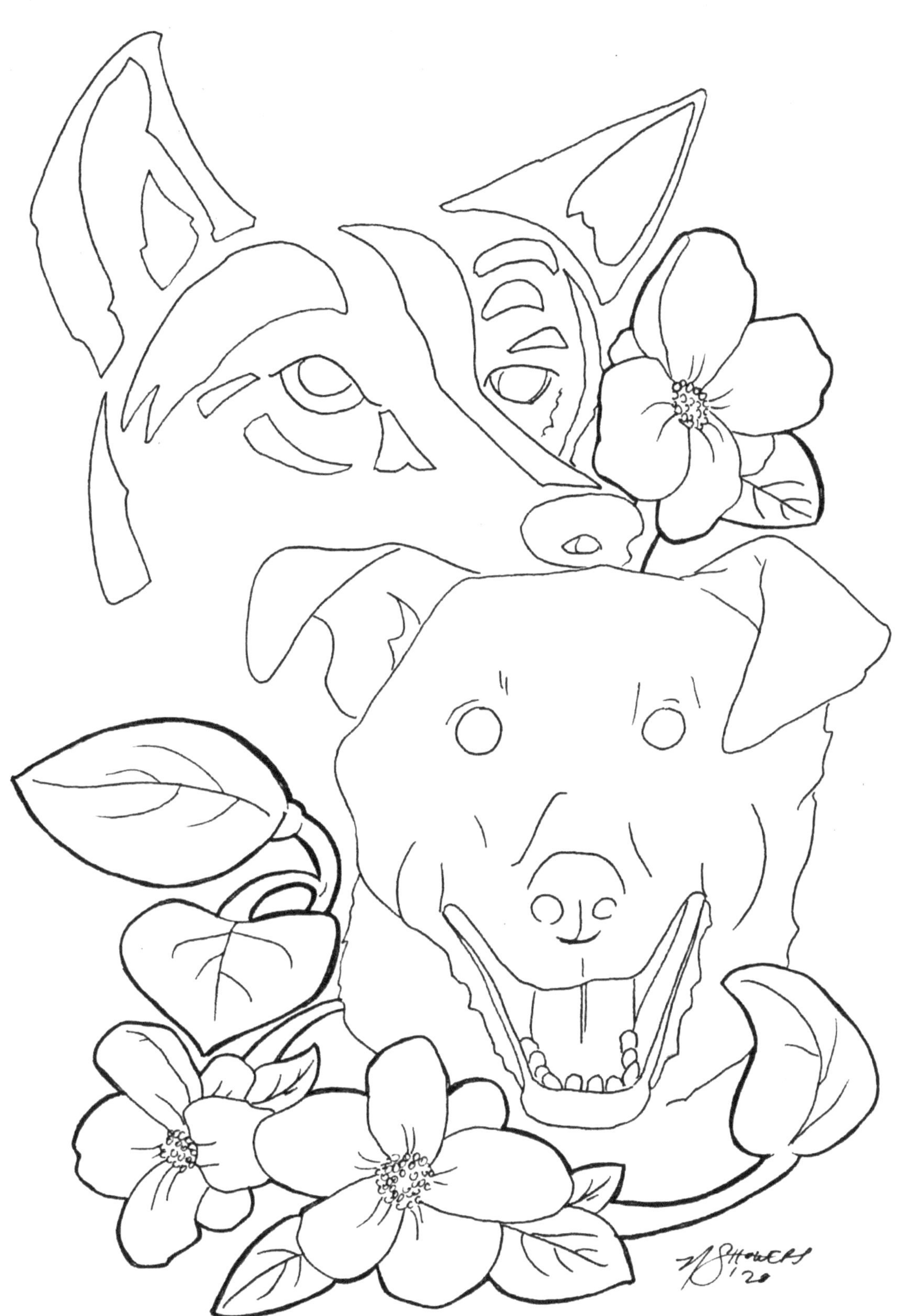
SHOWERS
'20

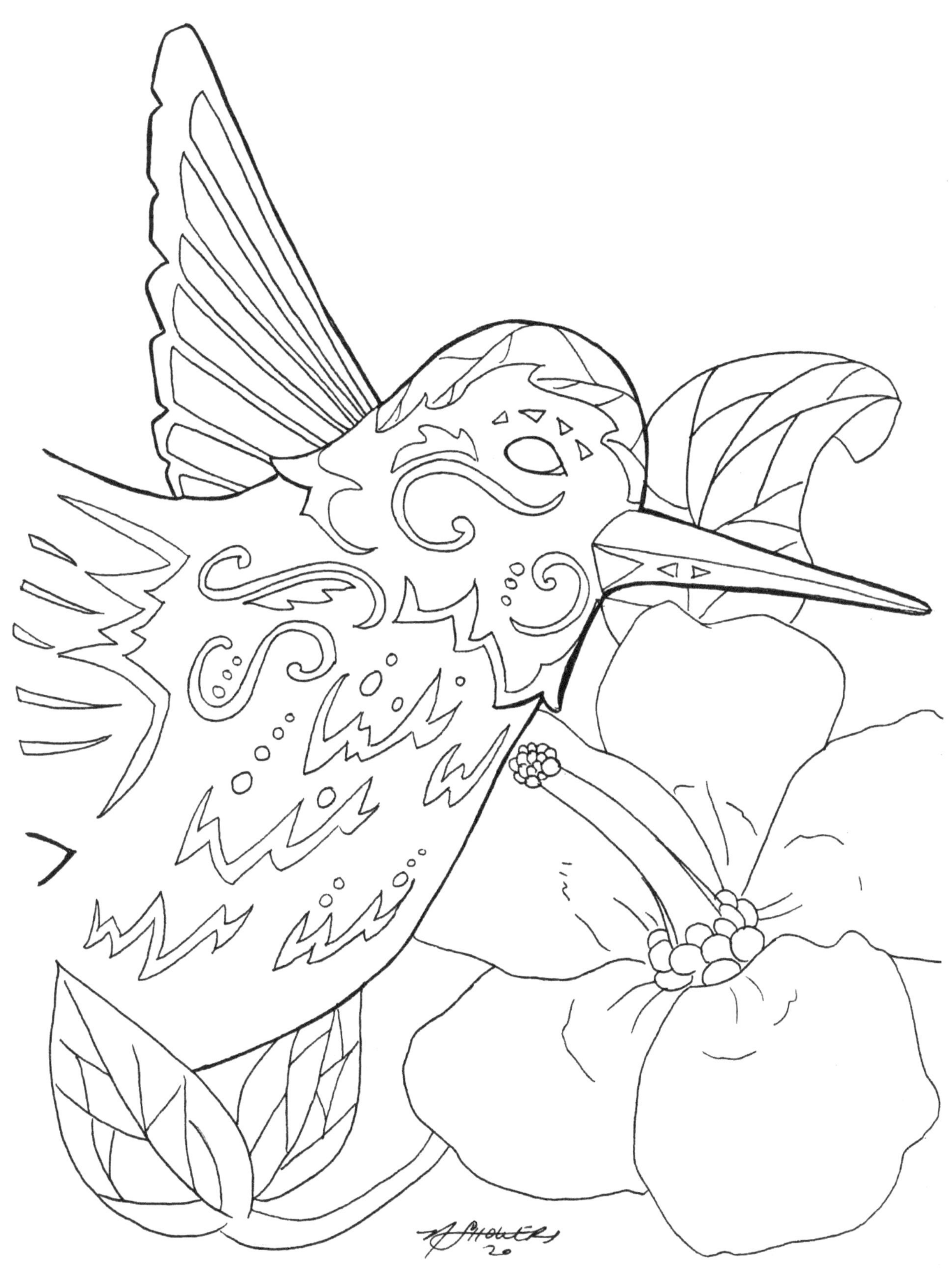

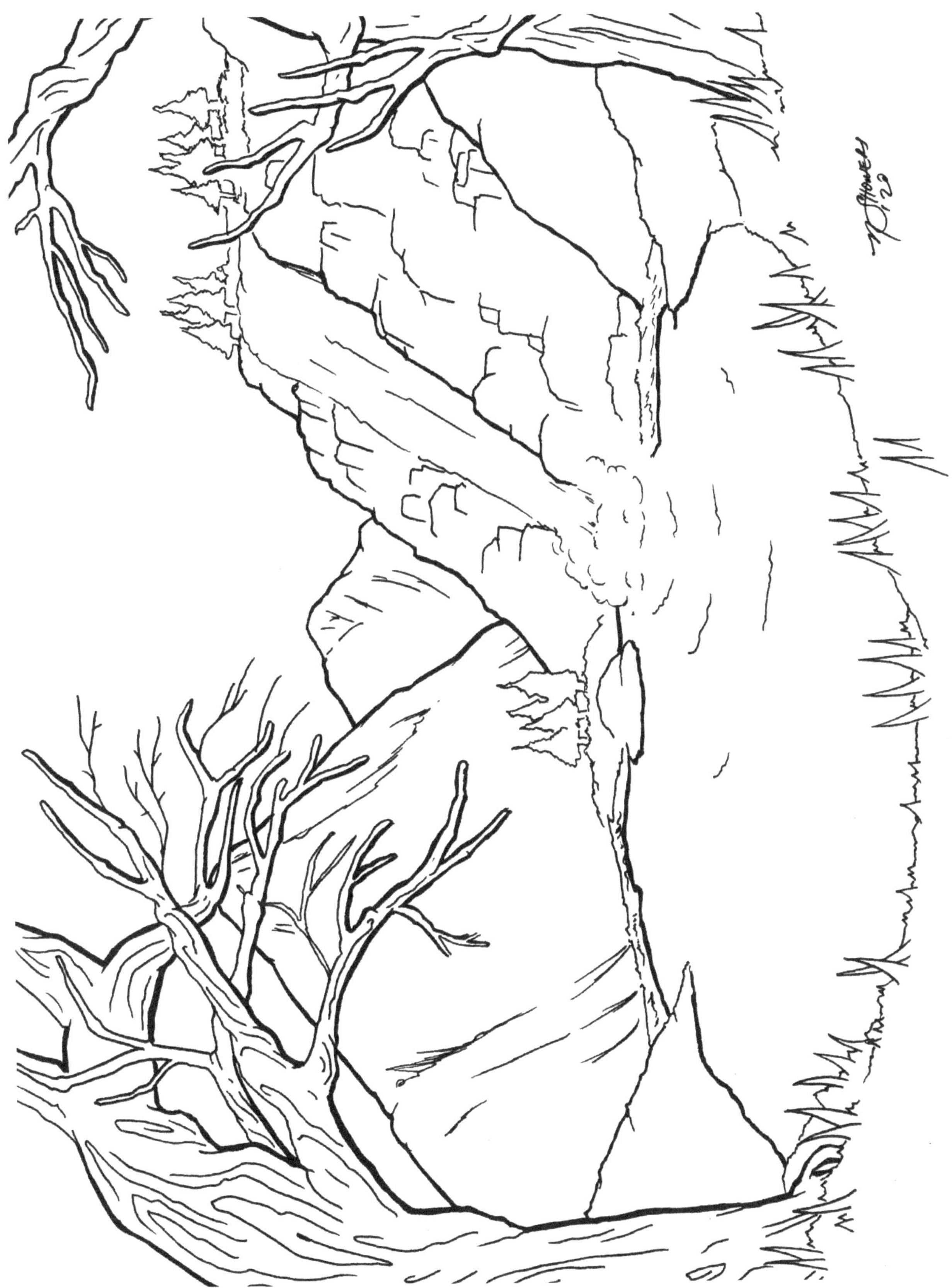

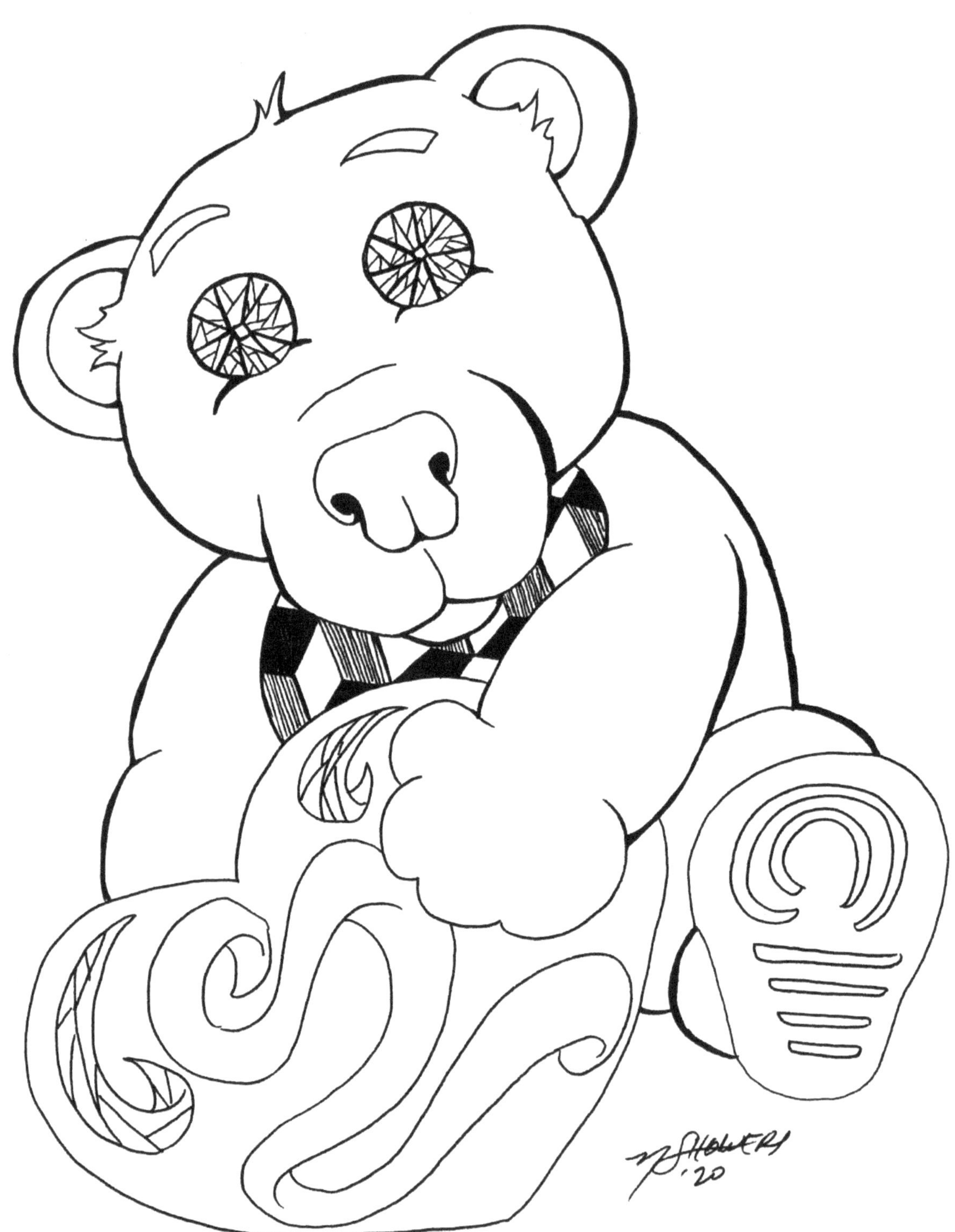

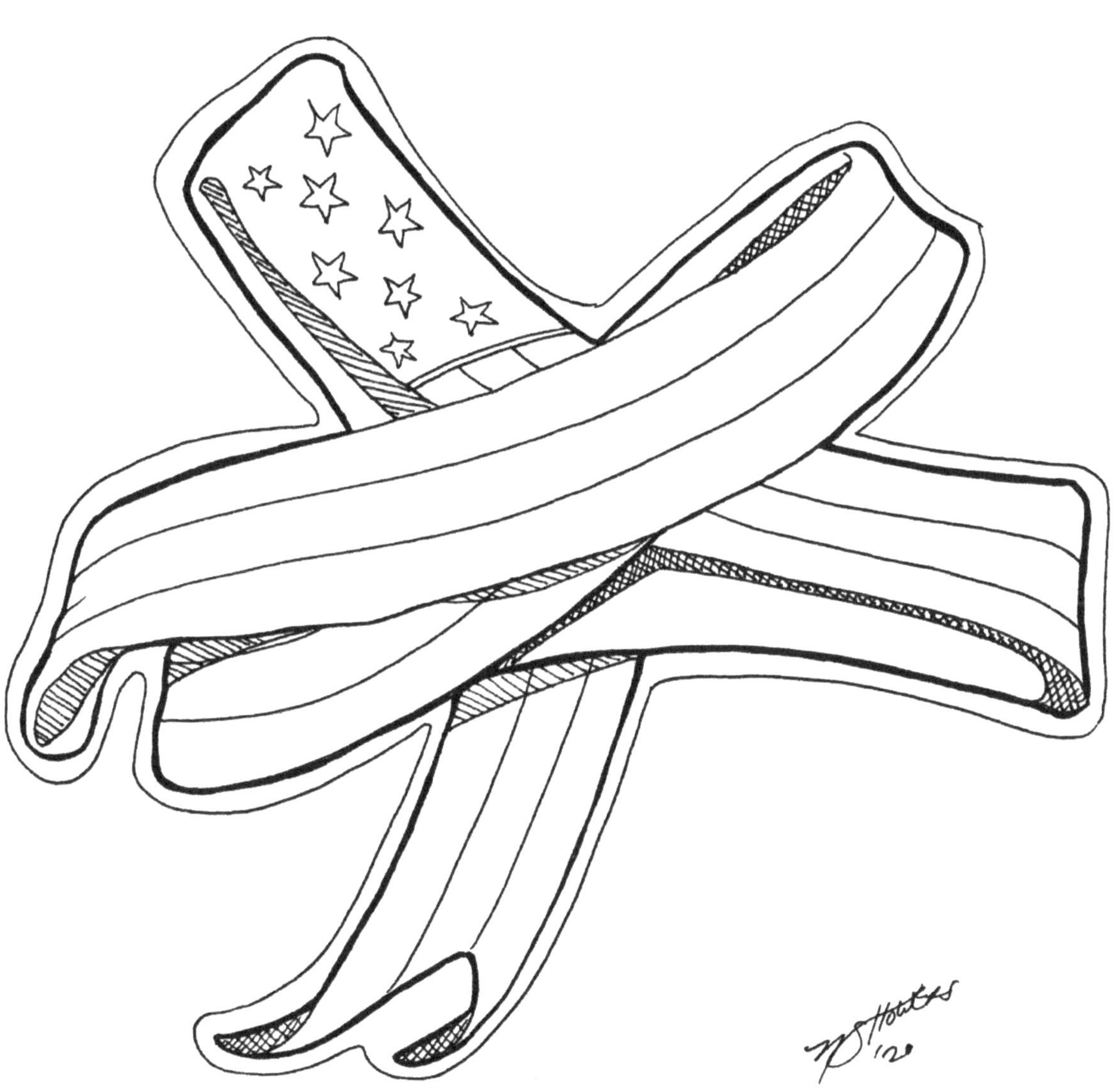

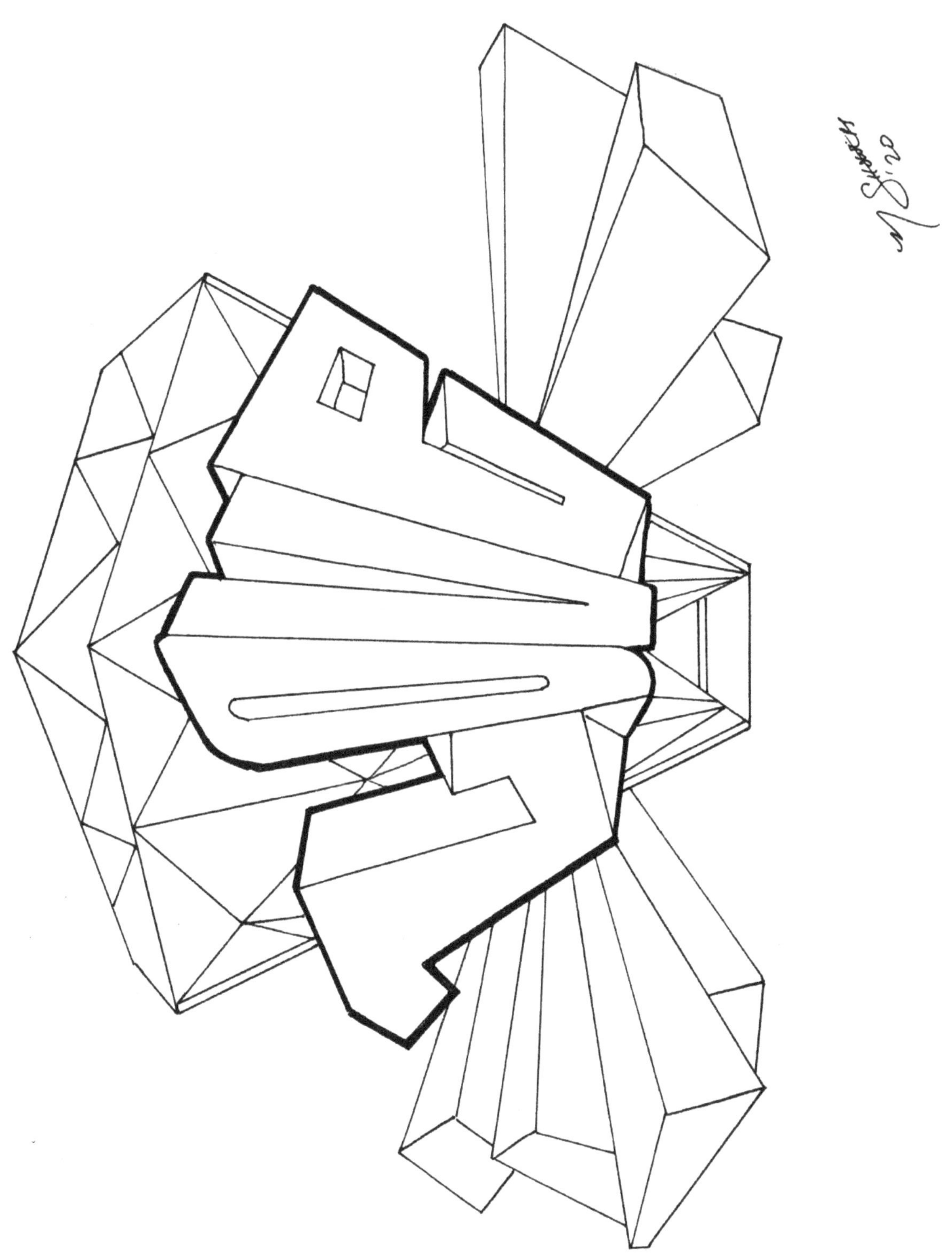

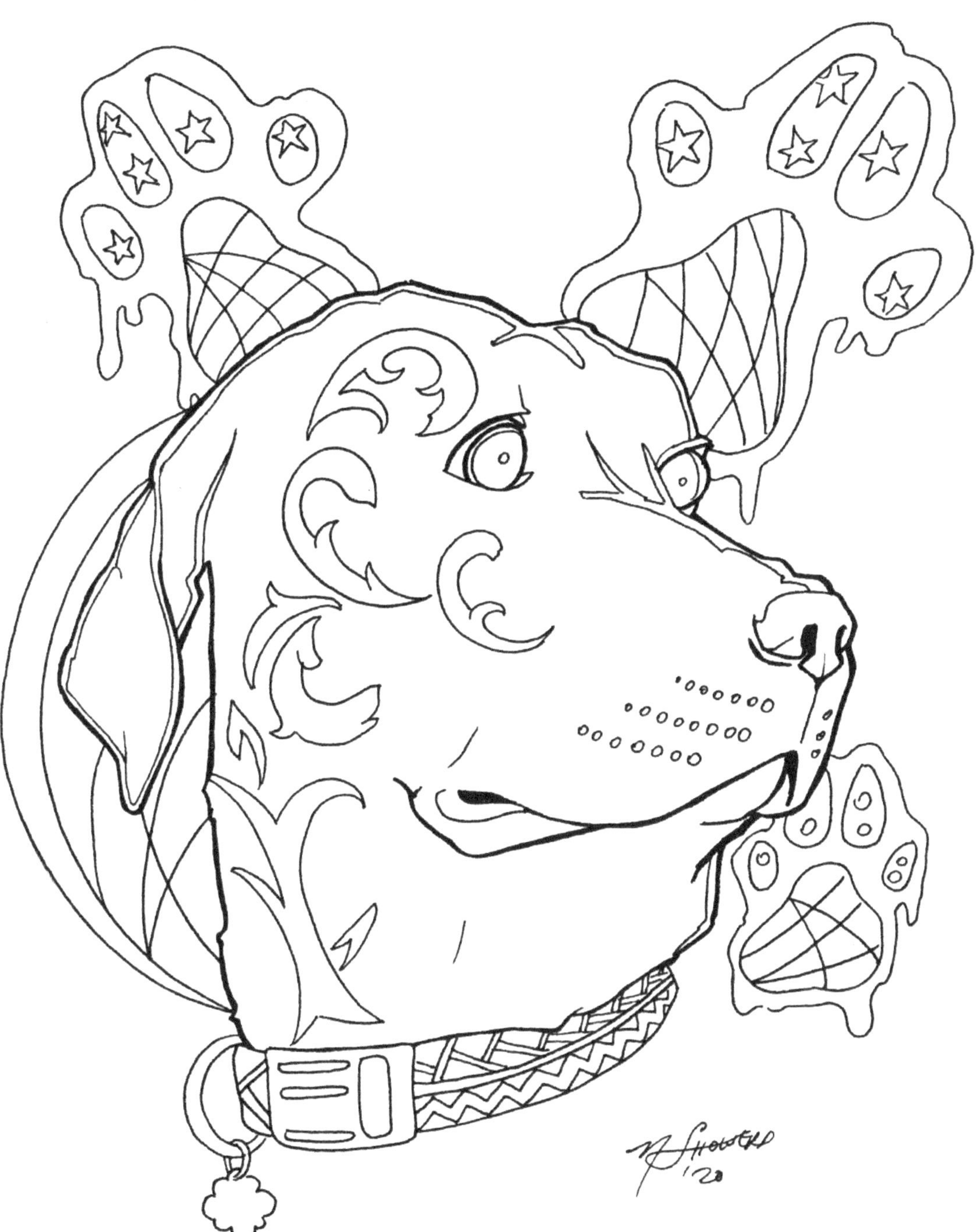

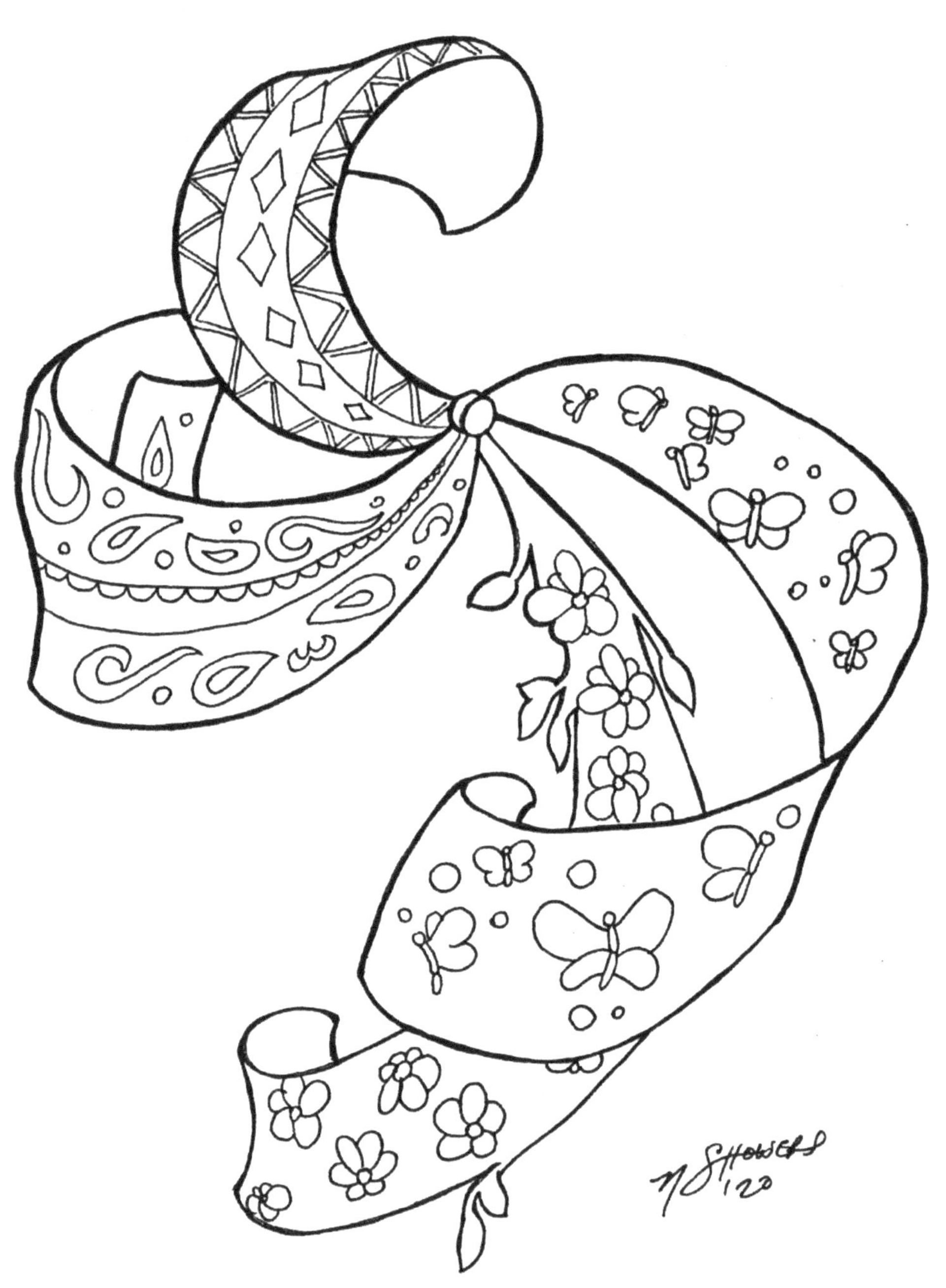
N SHOWERS
'20

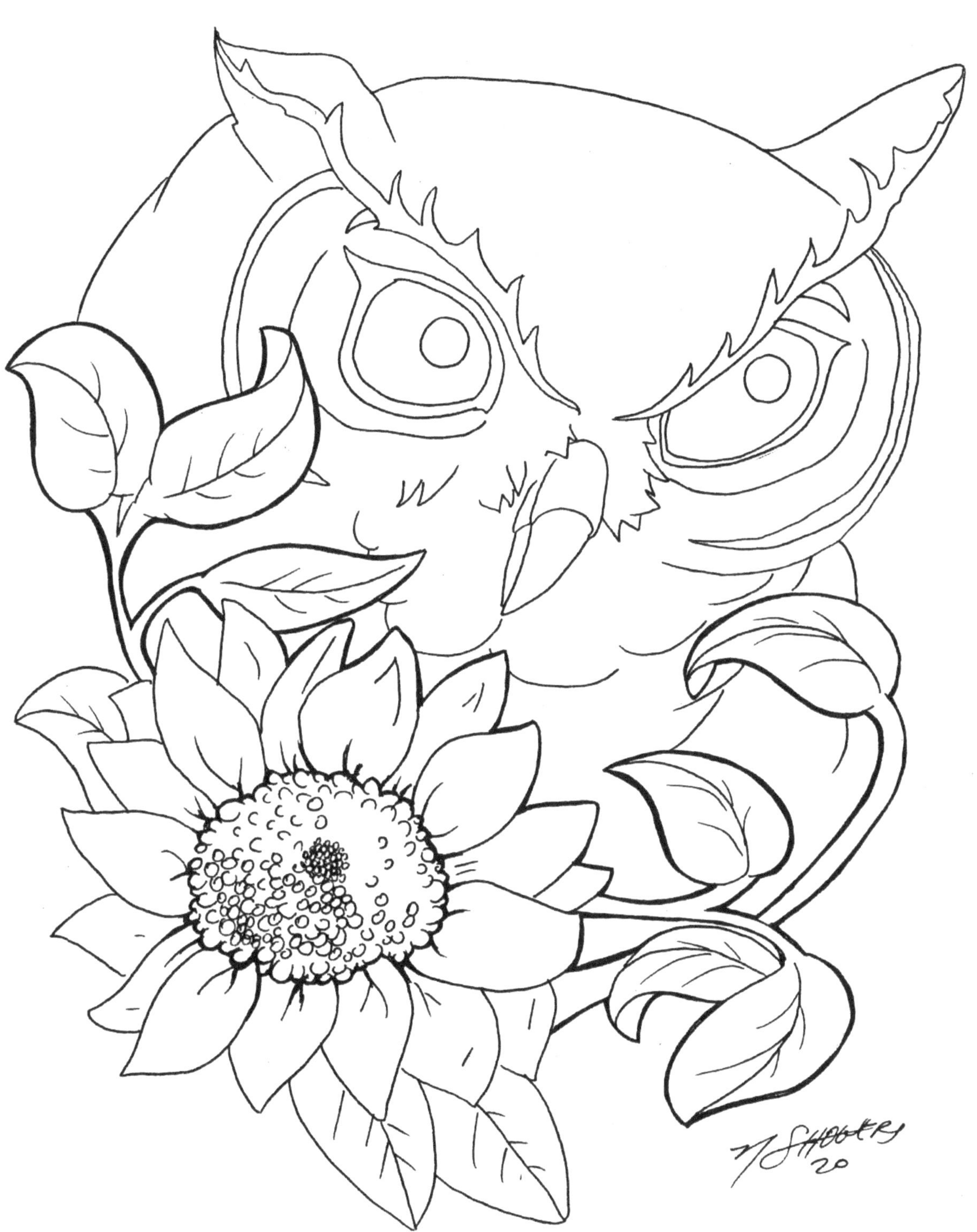

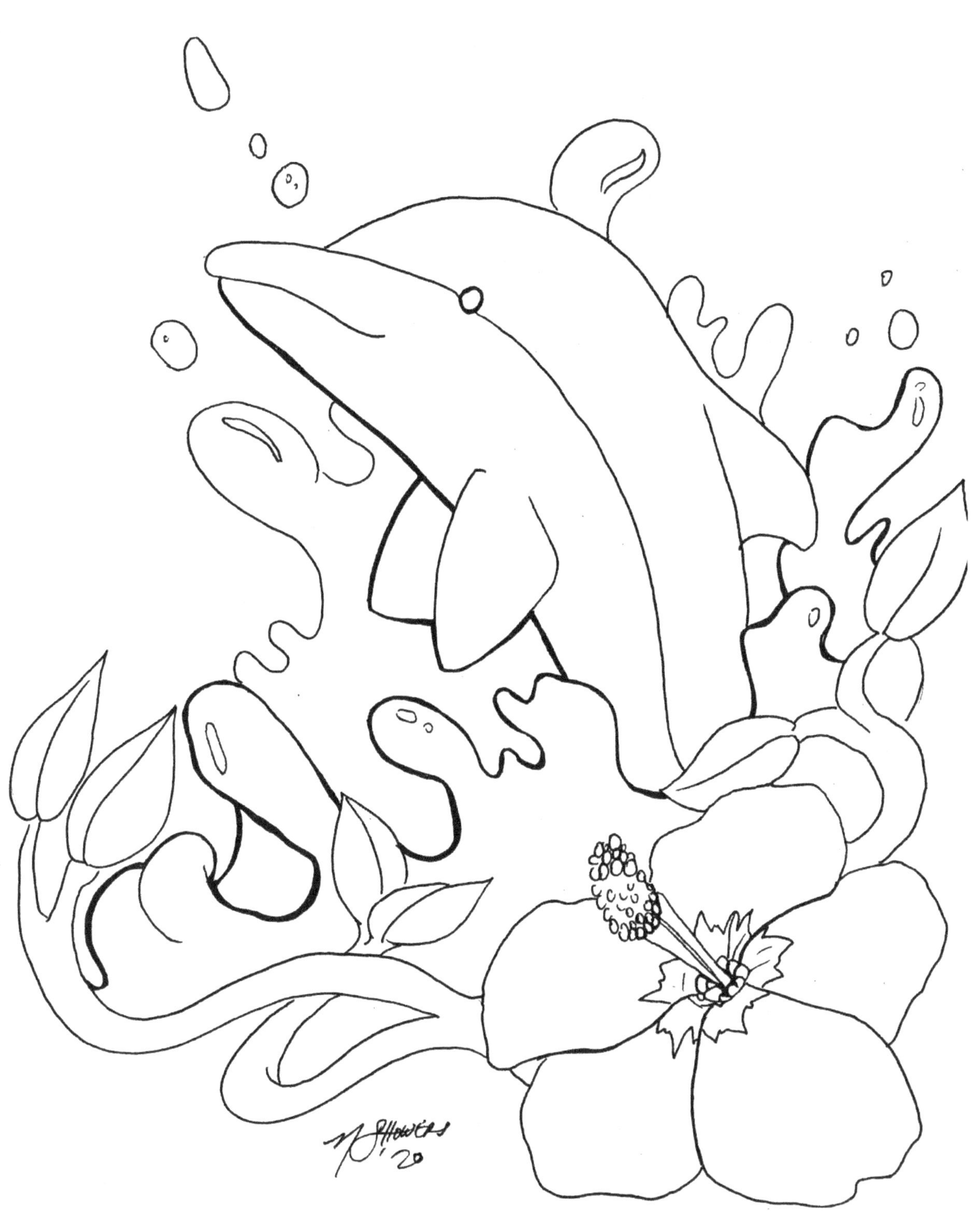

Use Your Imagination

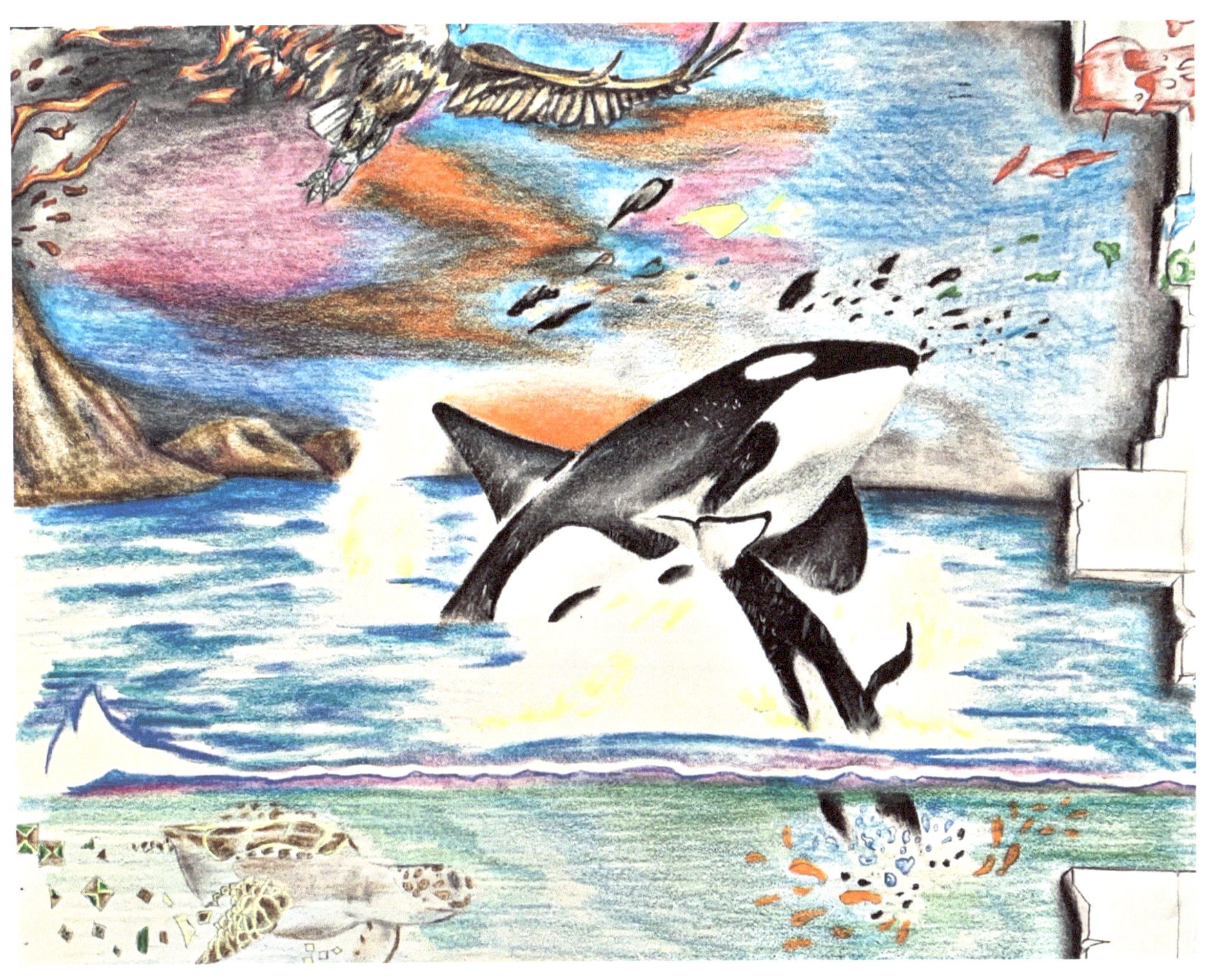

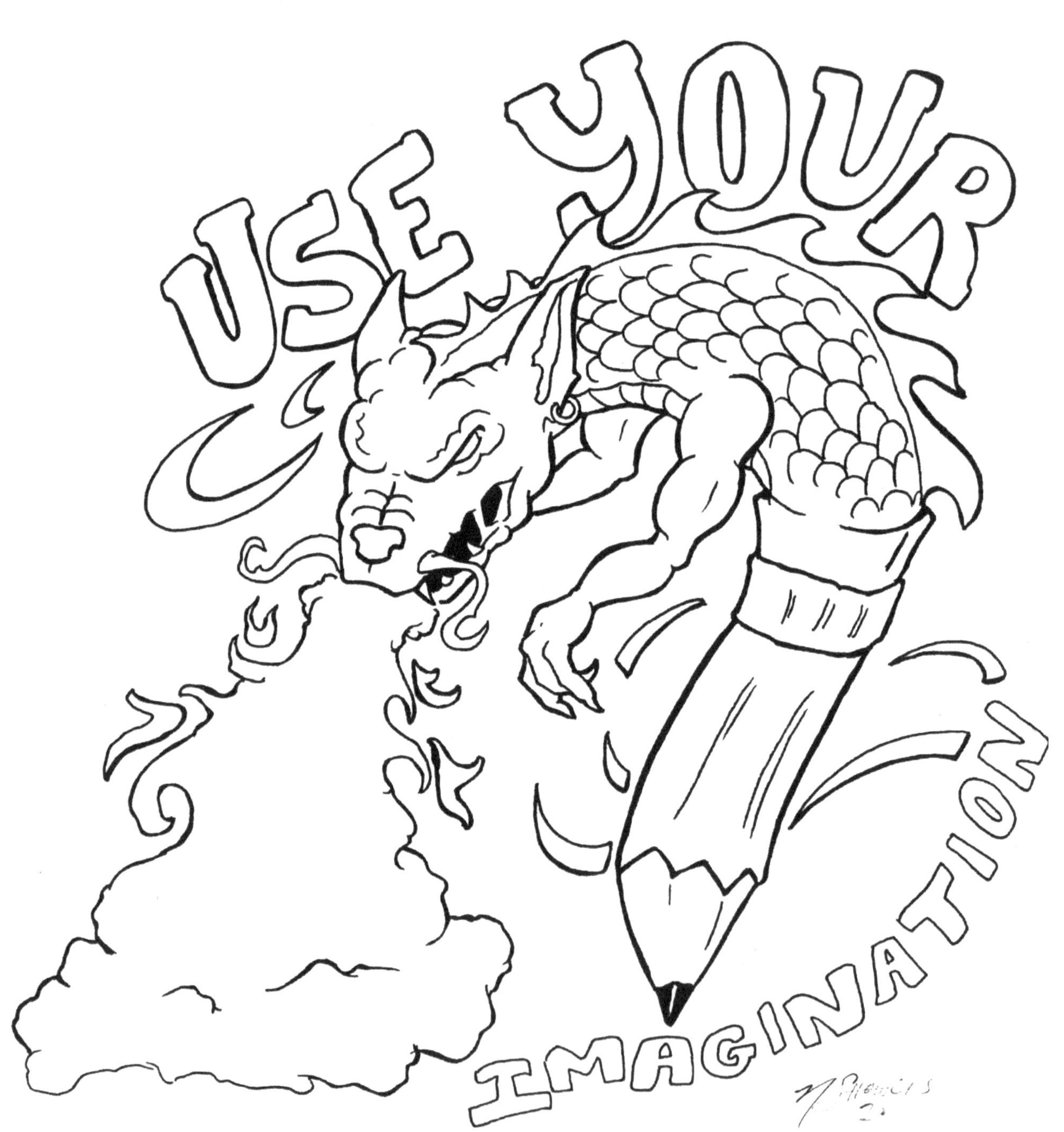
USE YOUR
IMAGINATION

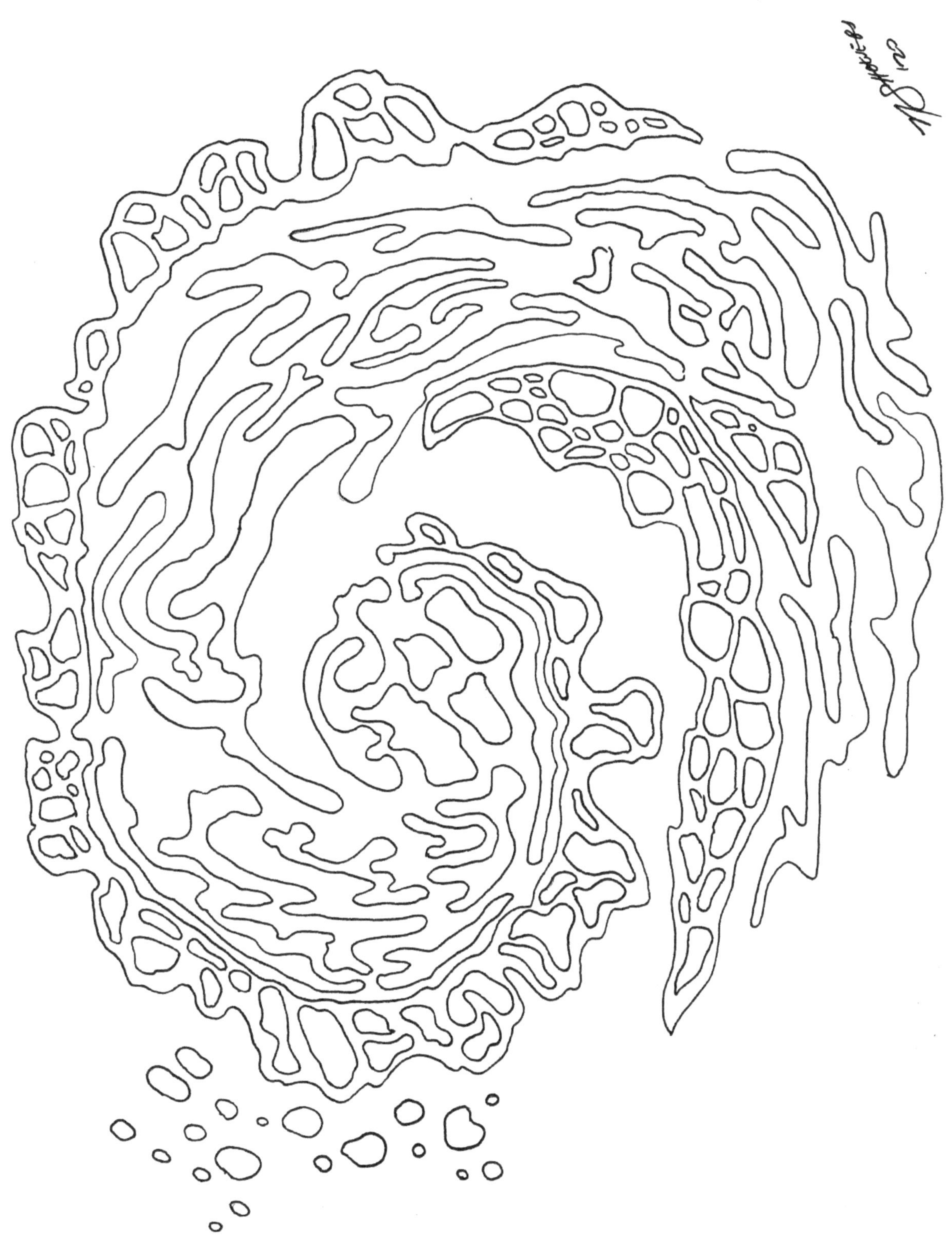

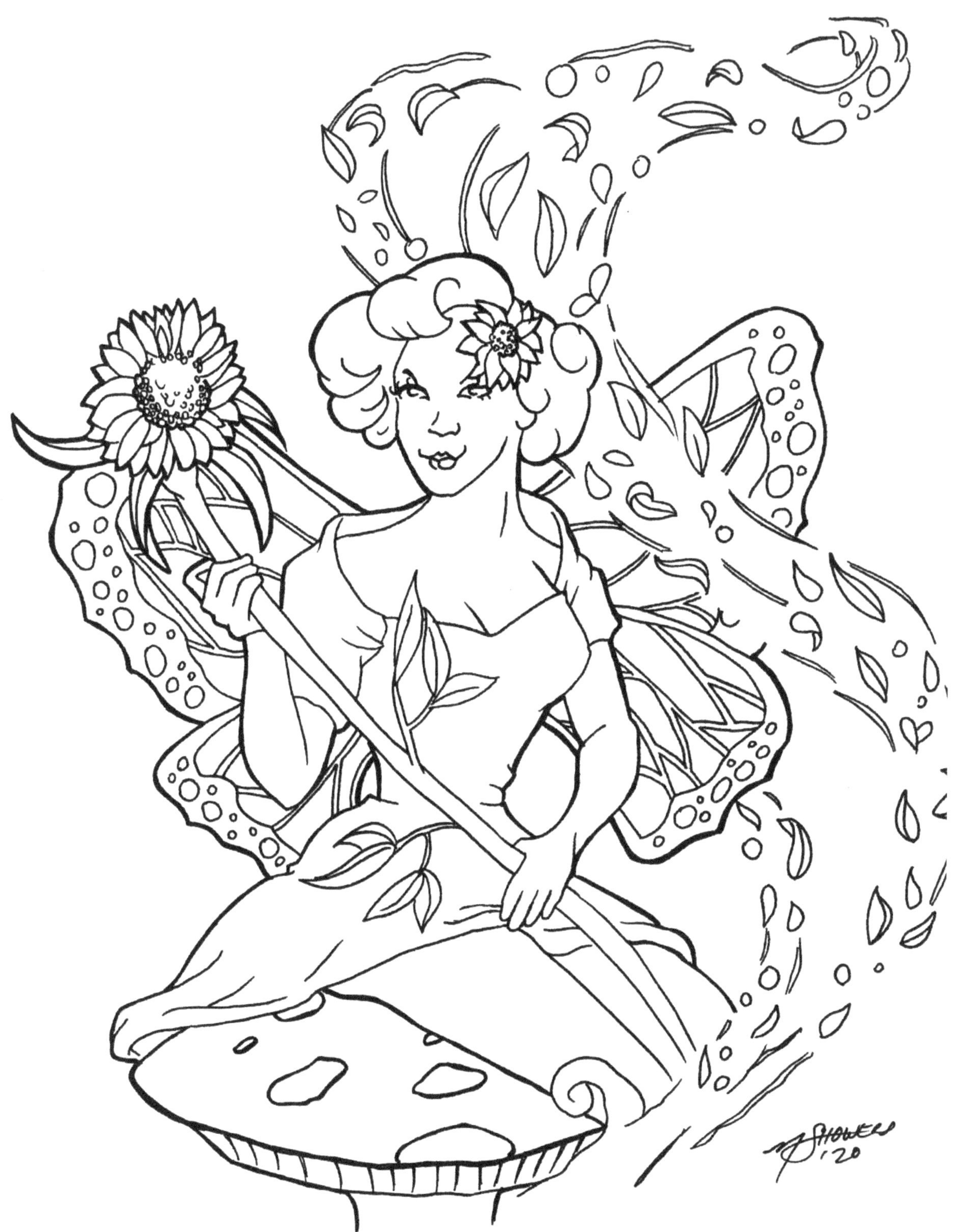

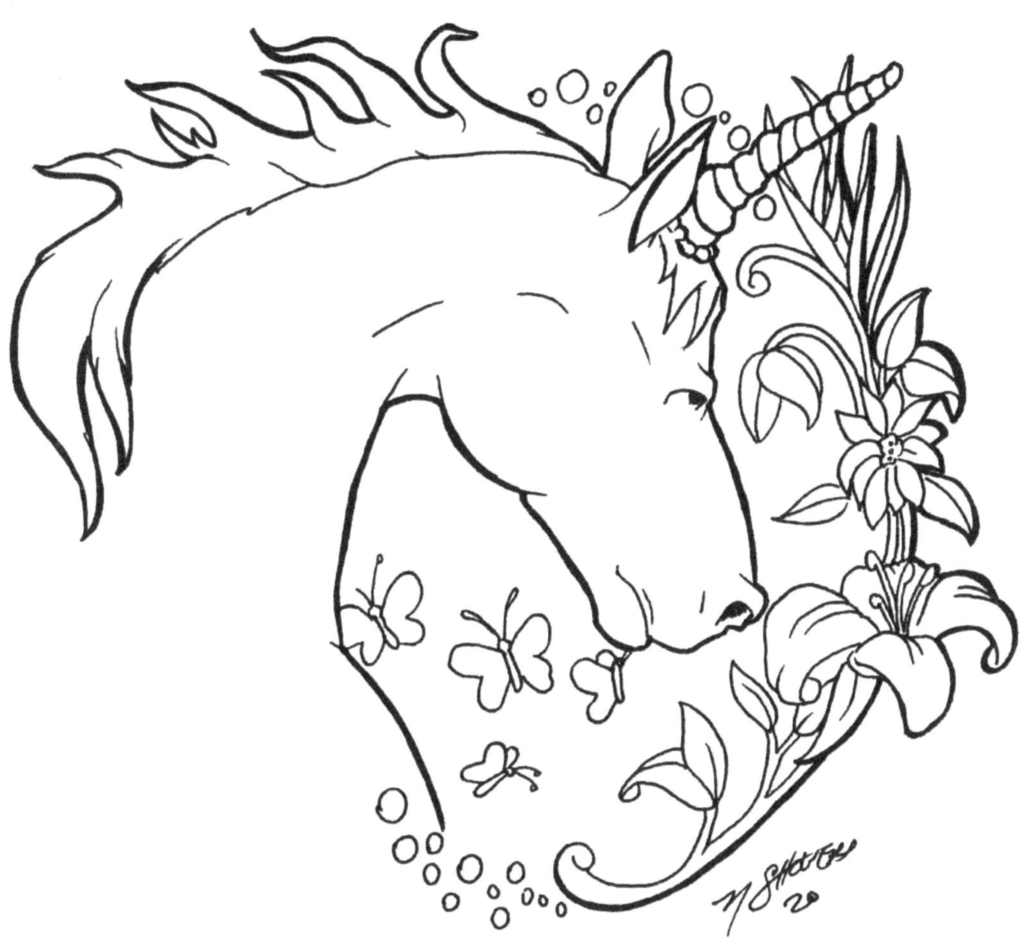

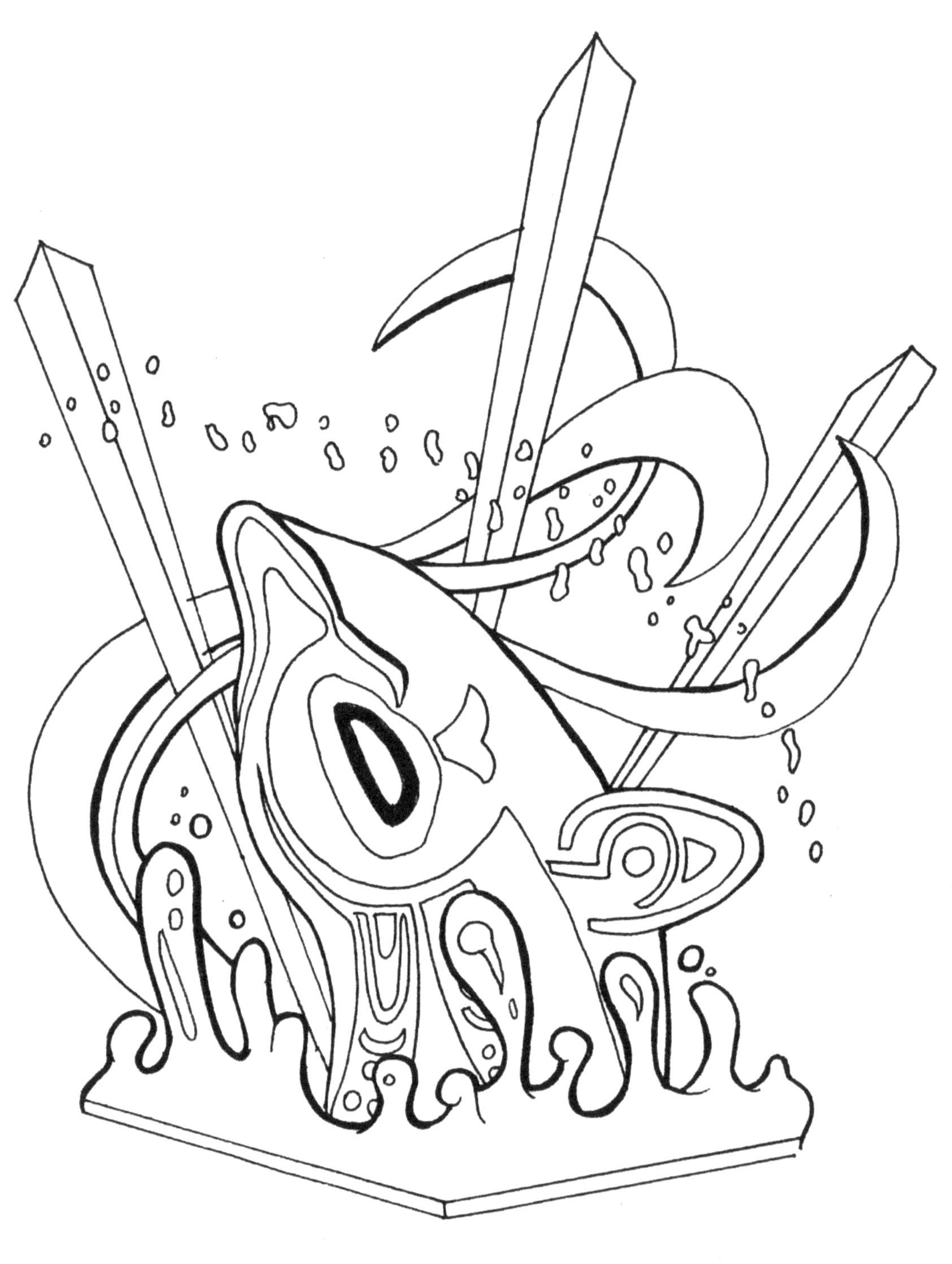
SHOWERS
'20

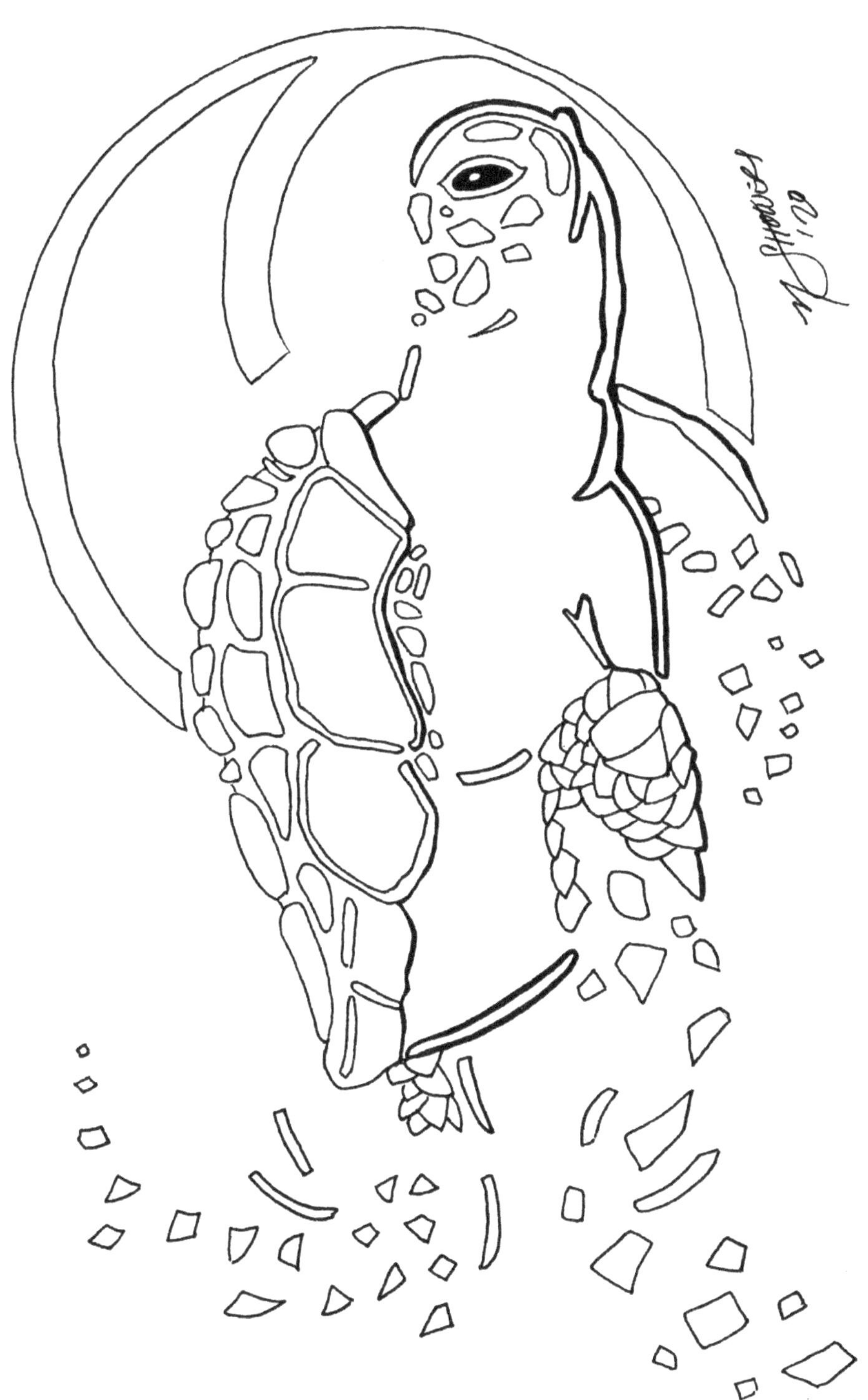

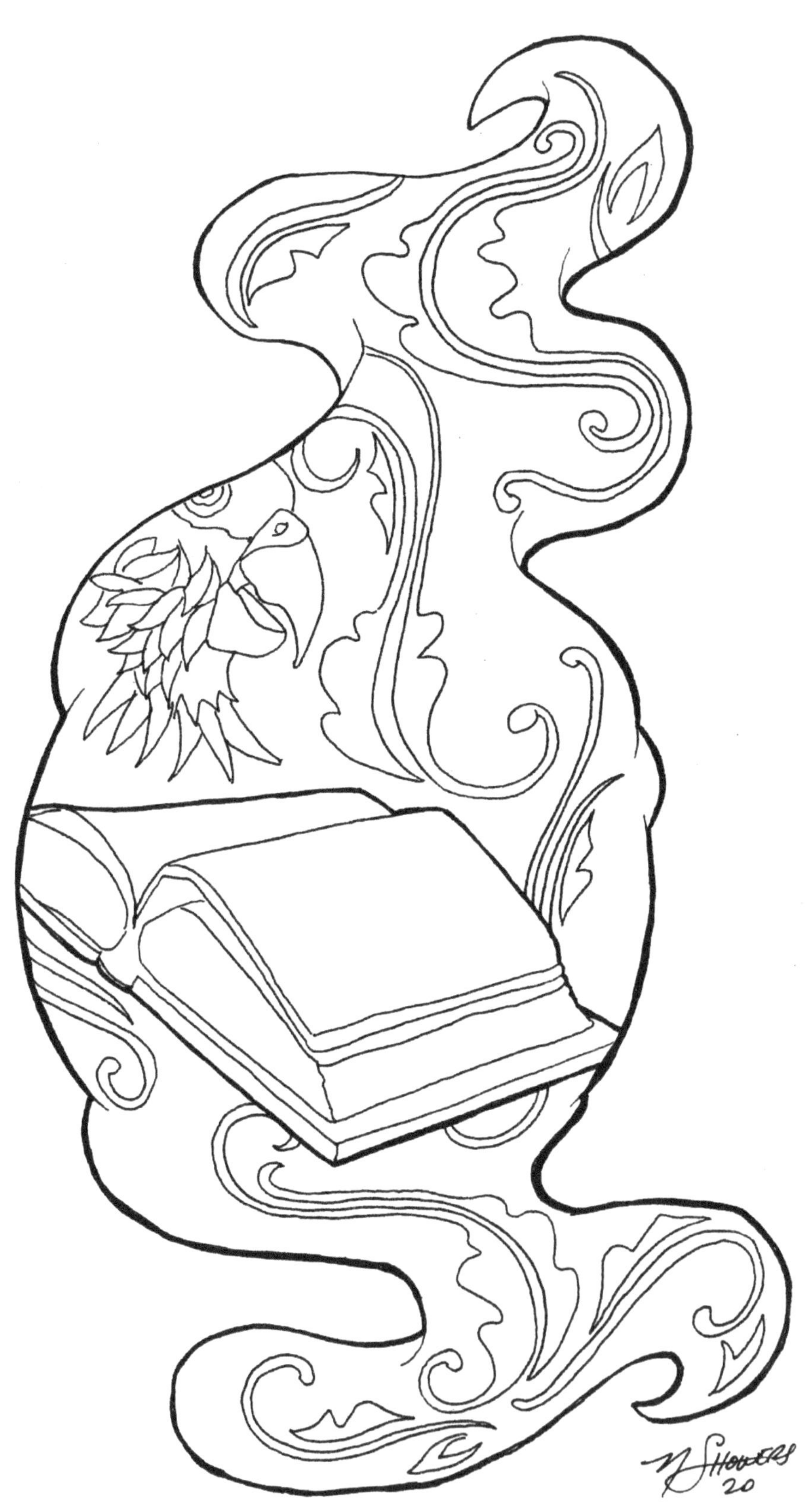

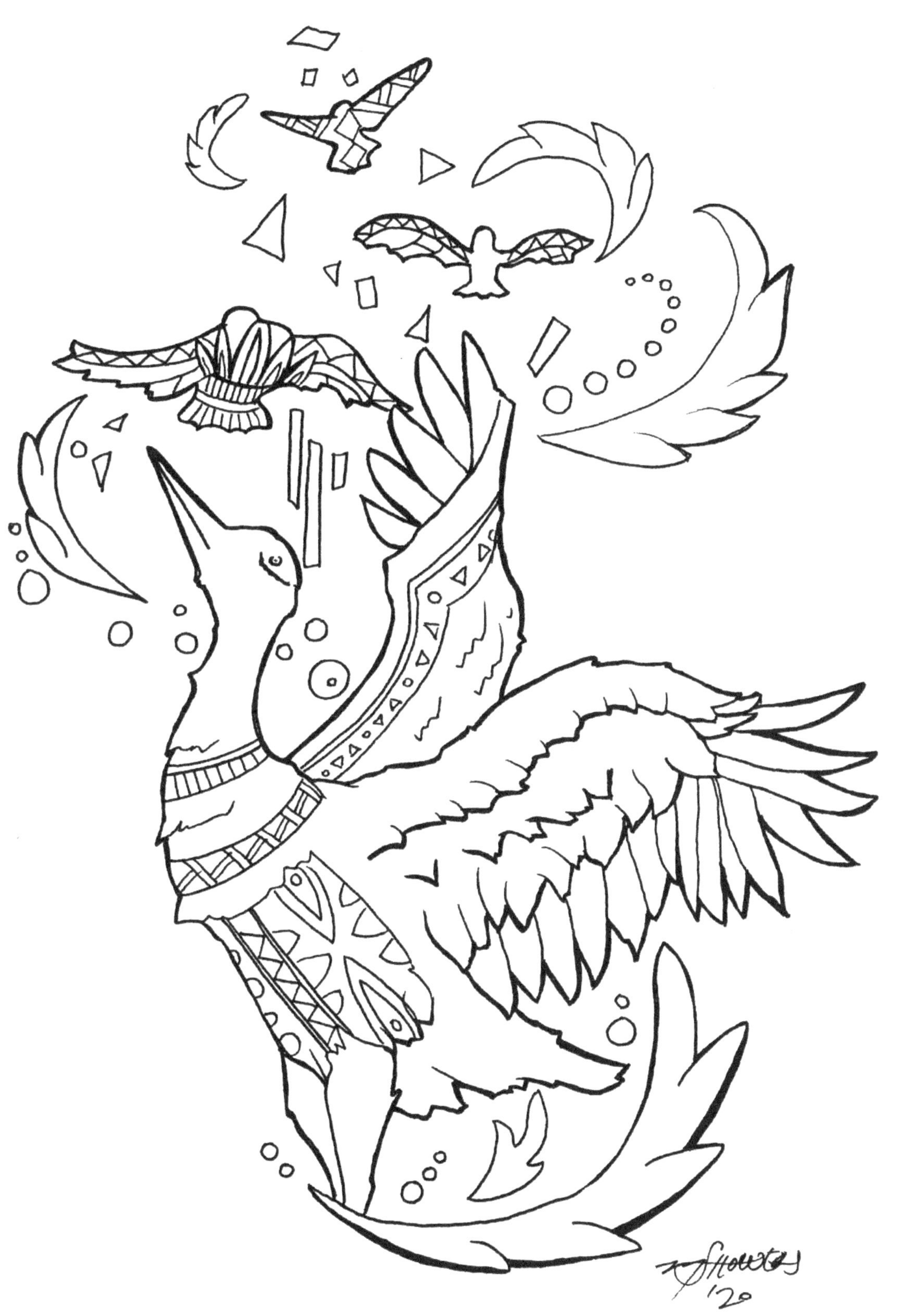

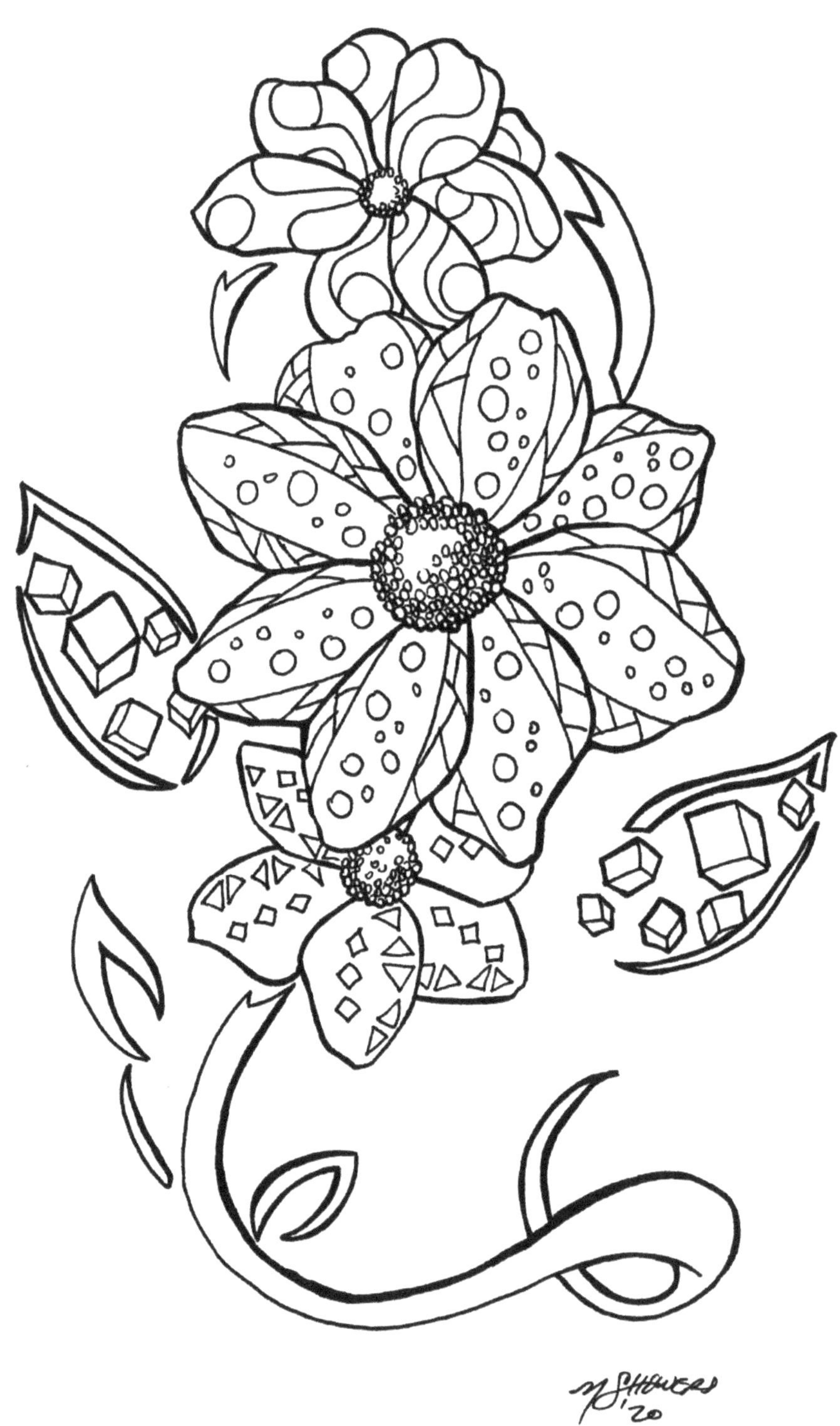
M SHOWERS '20

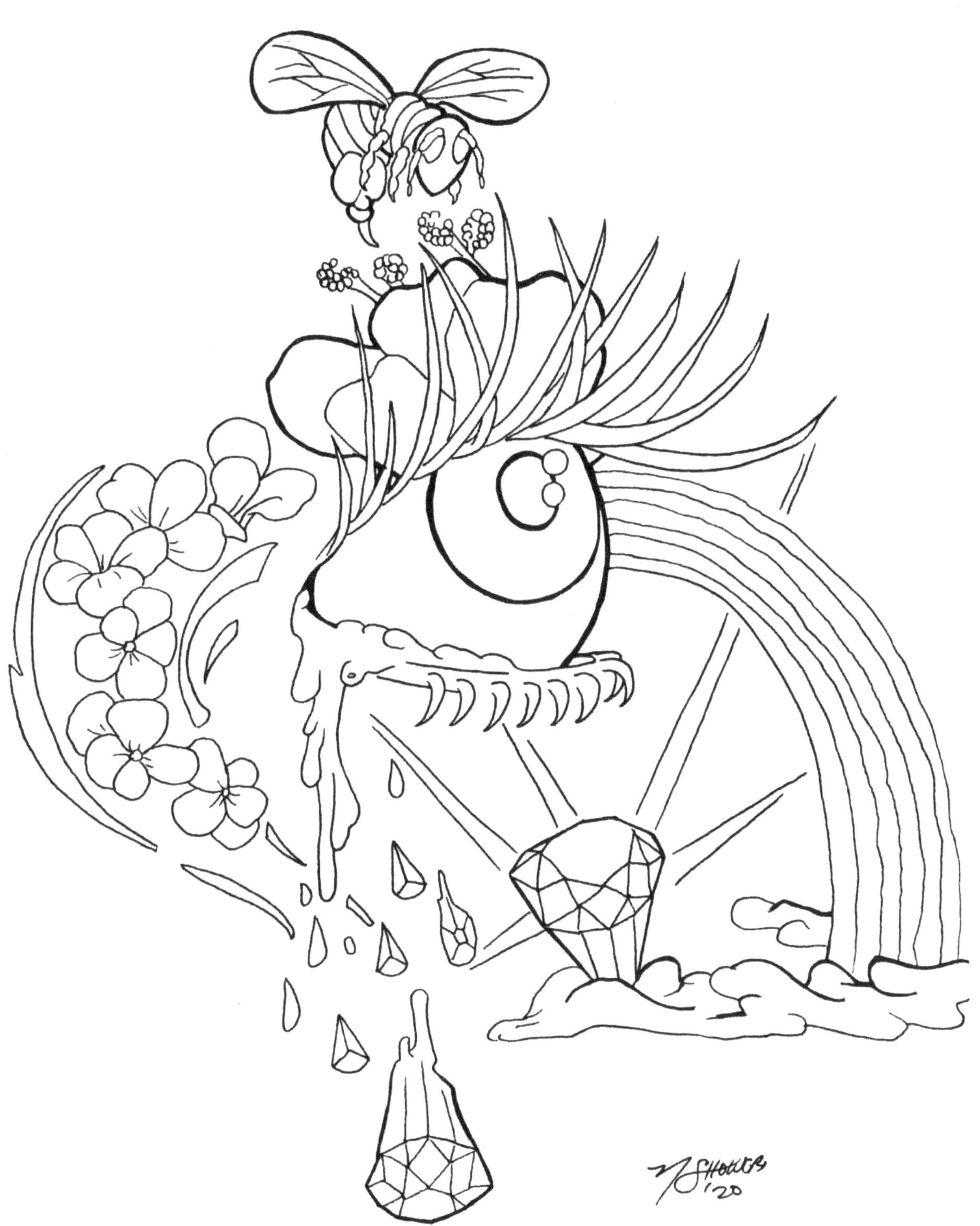

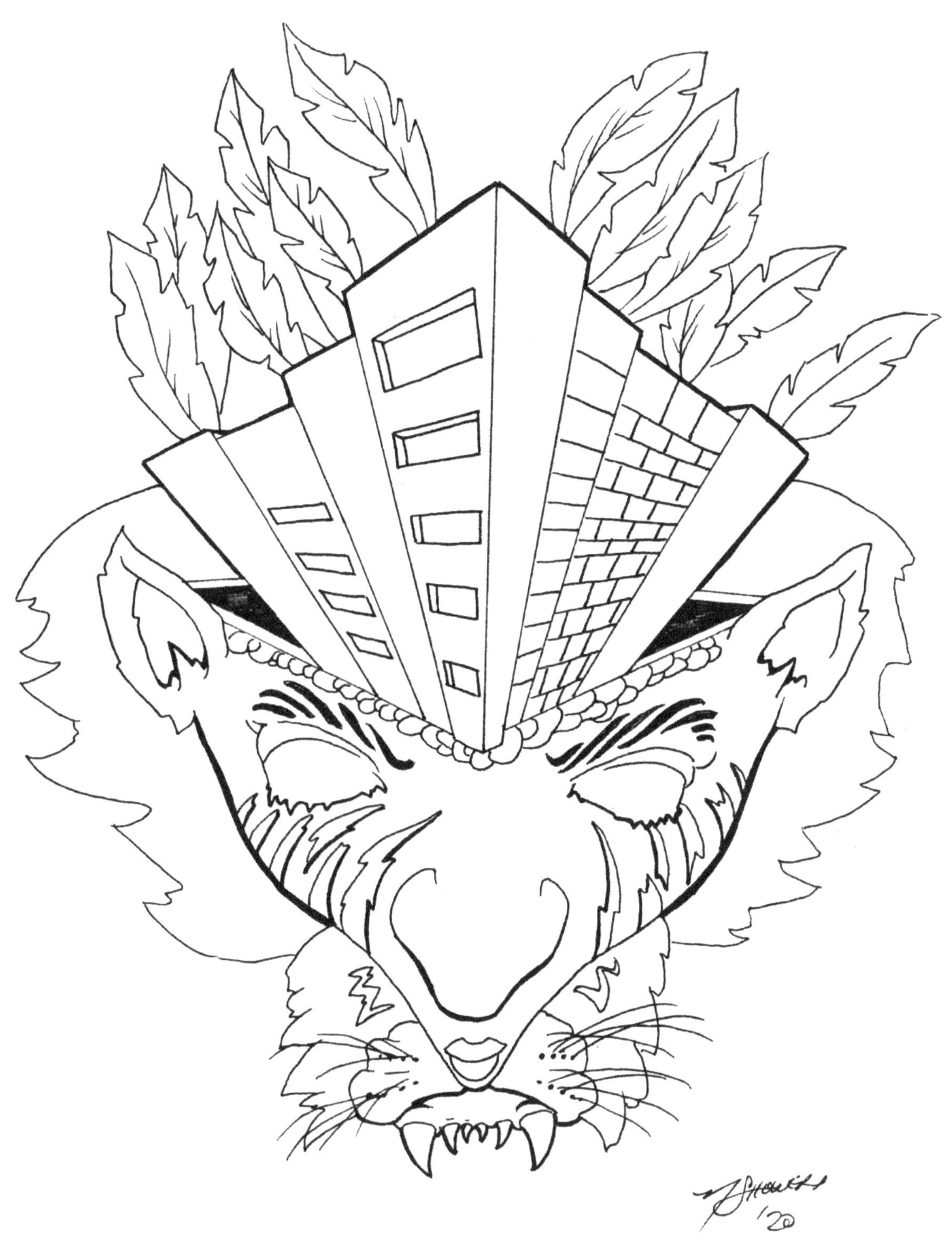

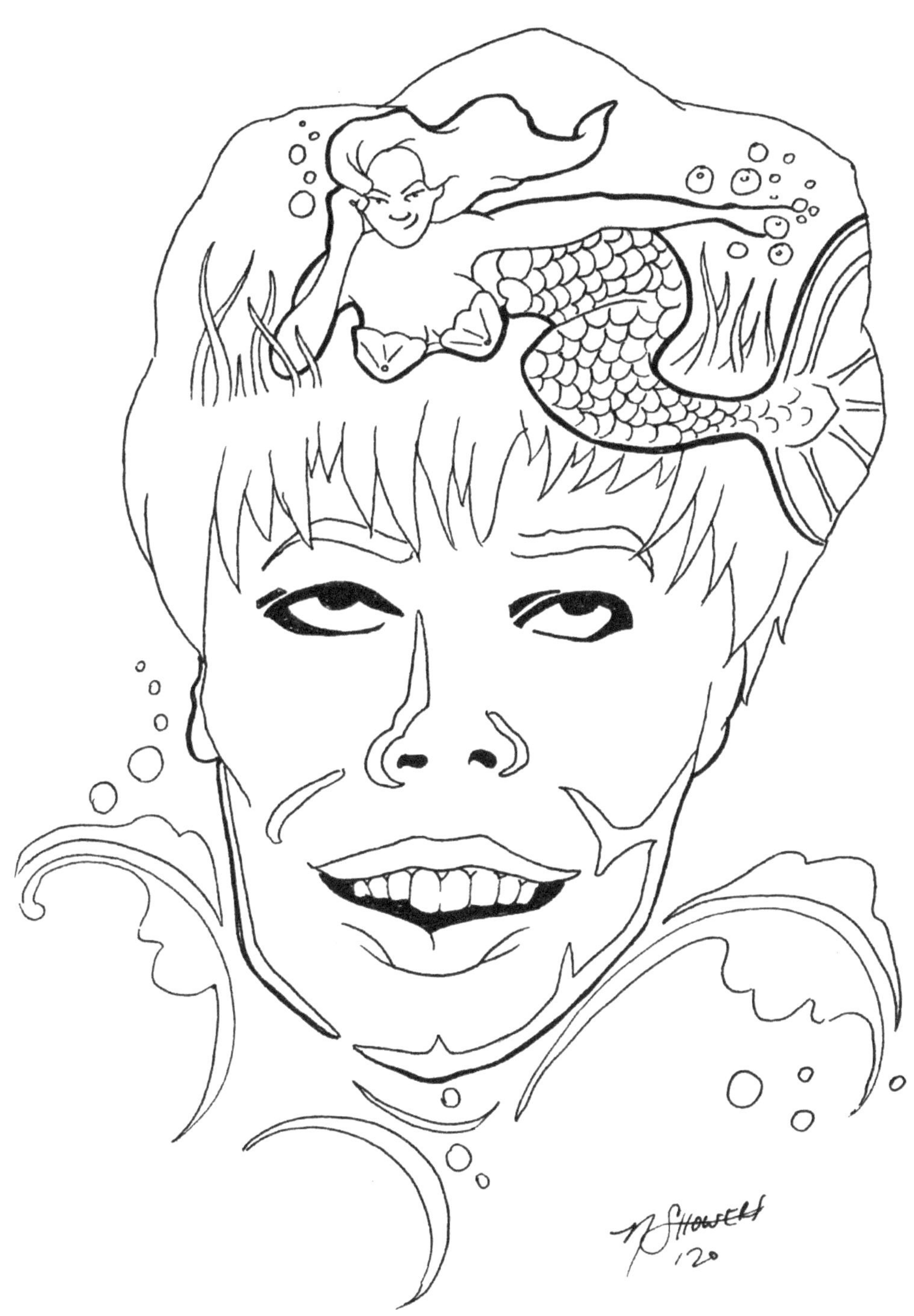

Express Yourself

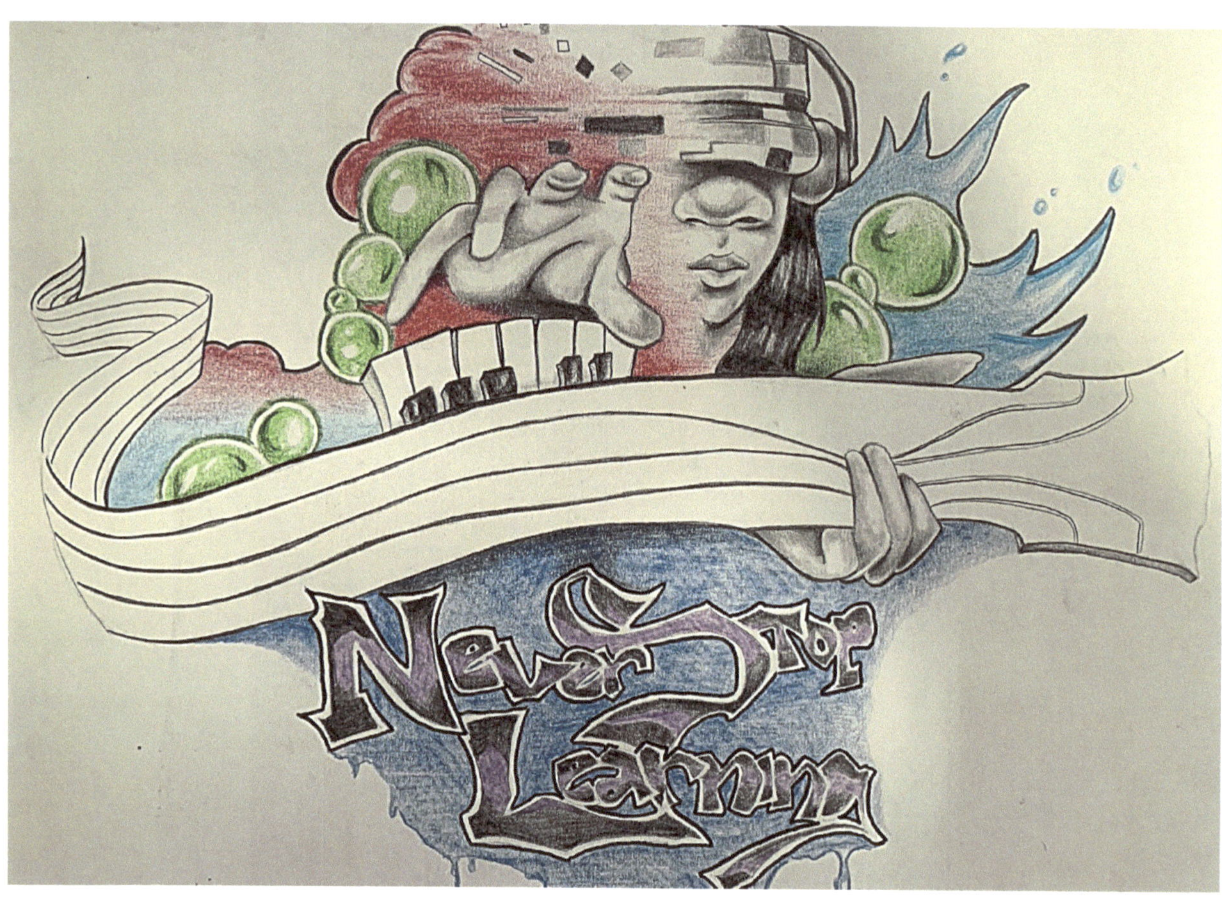

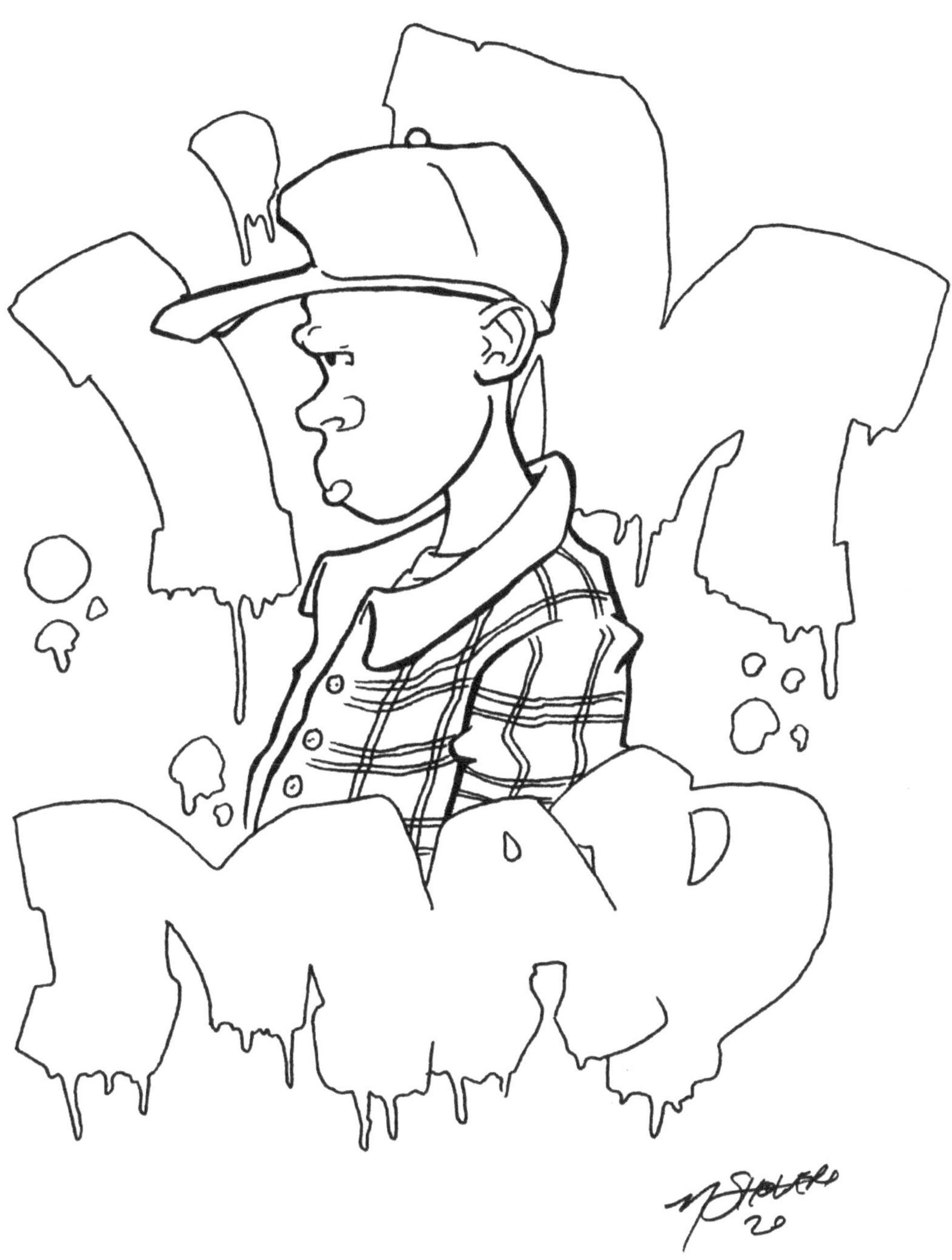

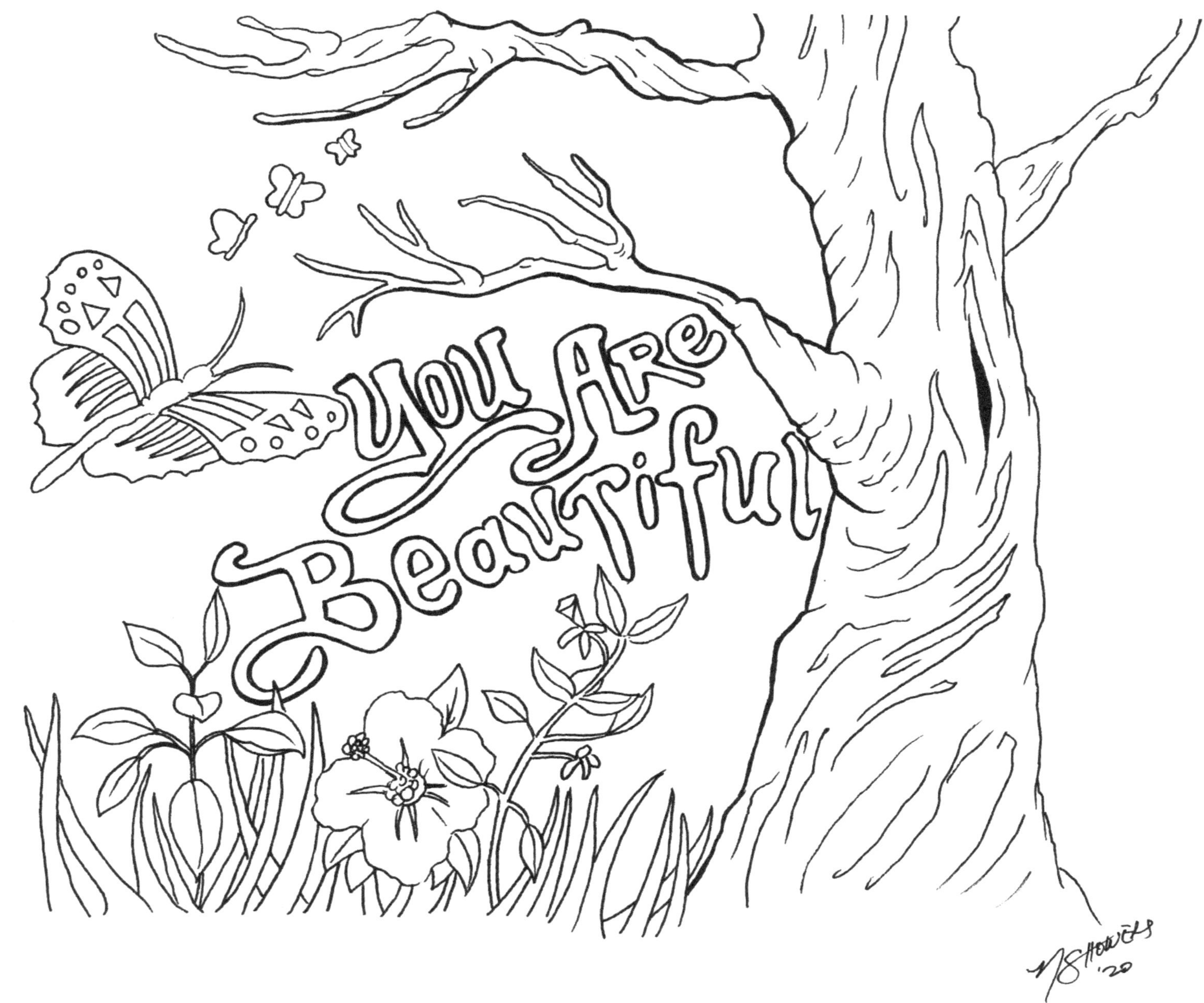
You Are
Beautiful

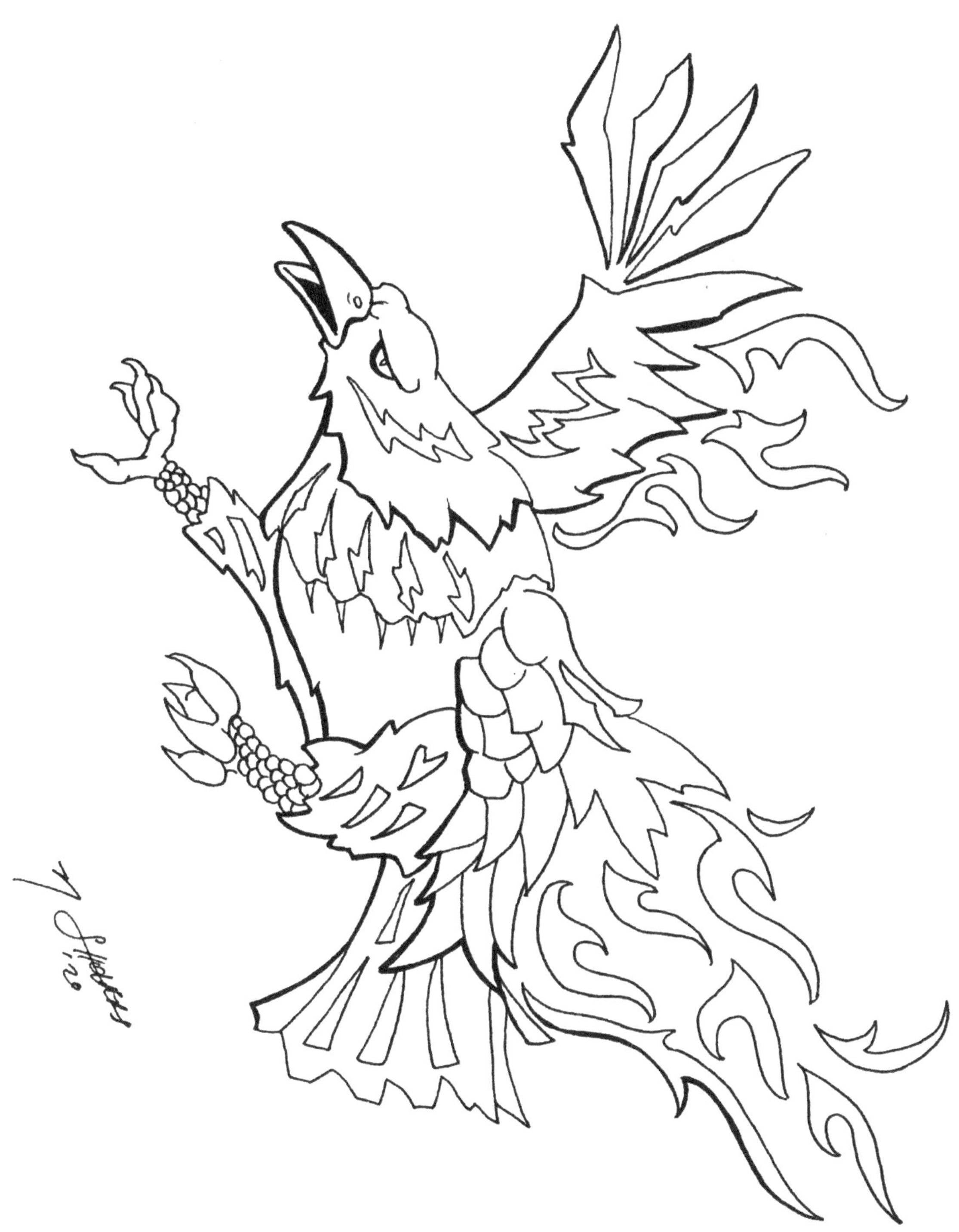

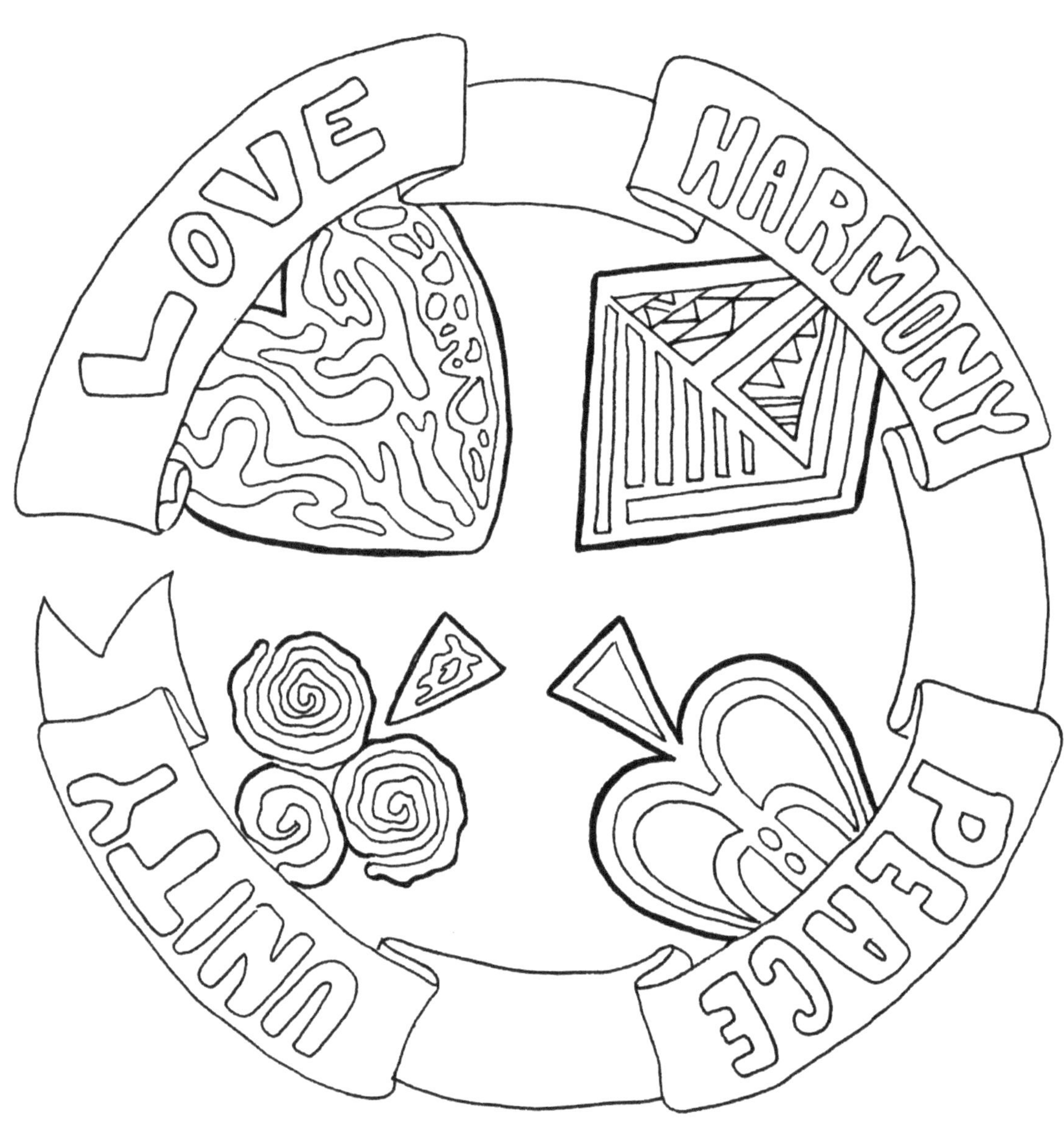

'20

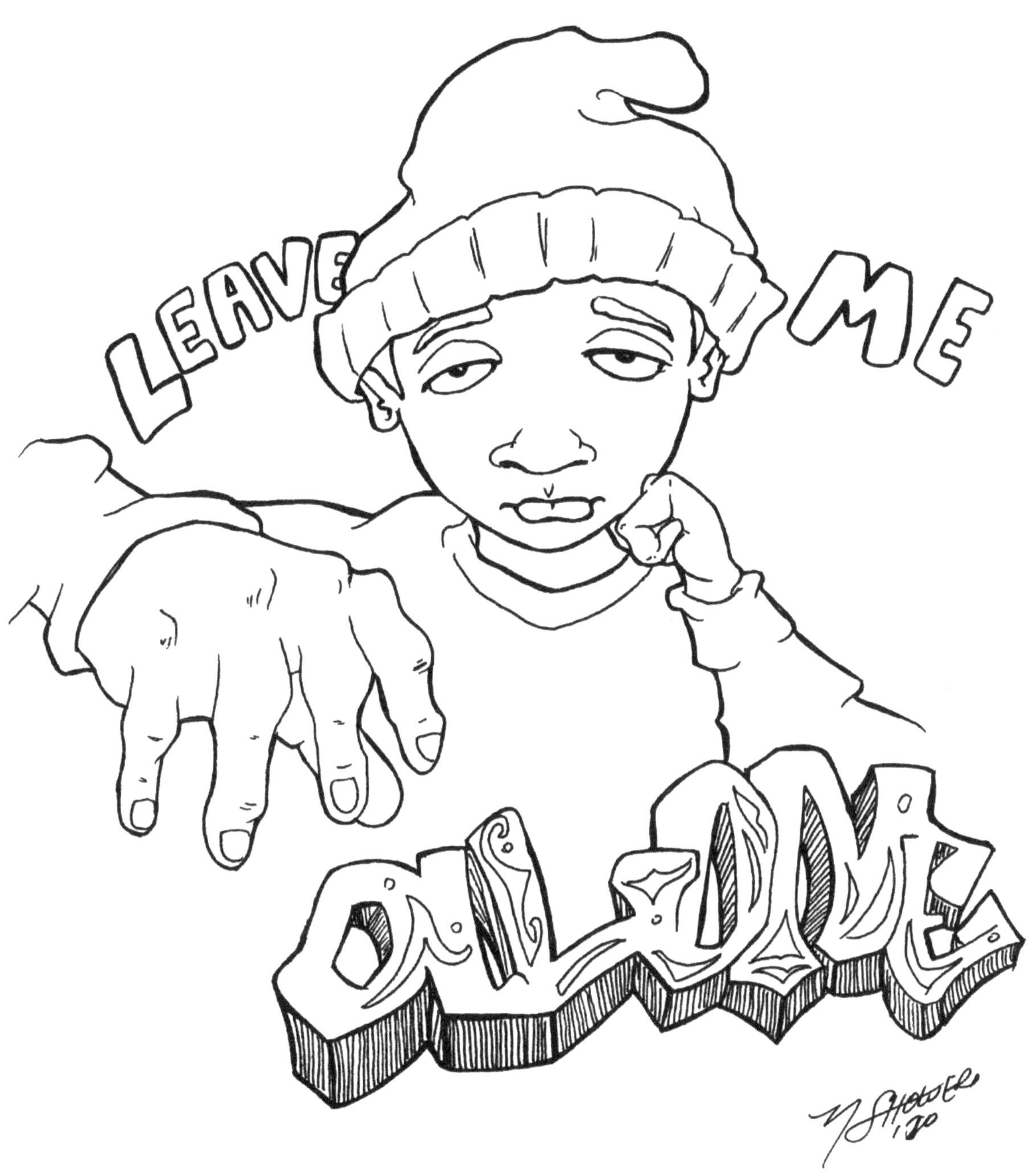
LEAVE
ME

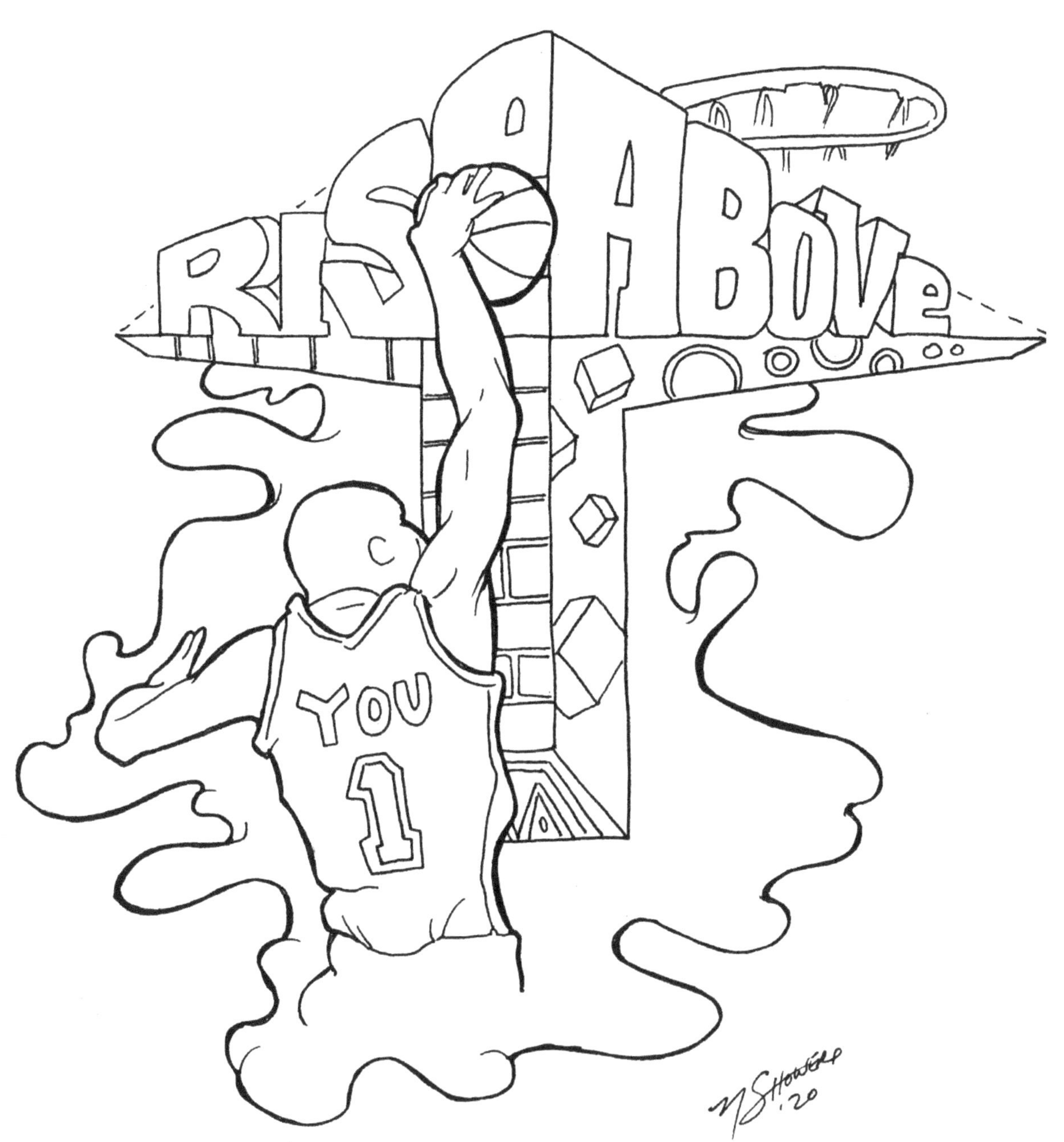
ABOVE
YOU
1

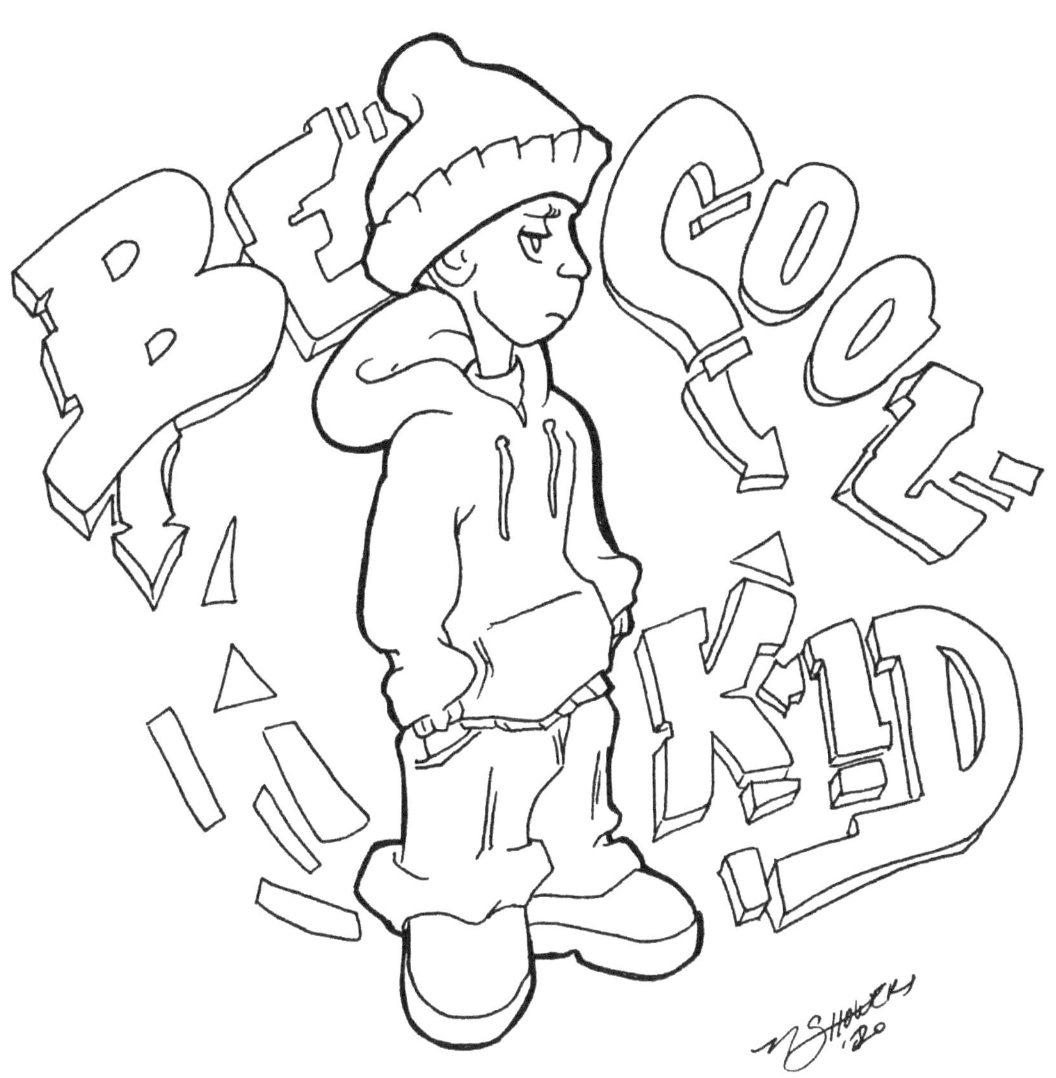
BE COOL
KID

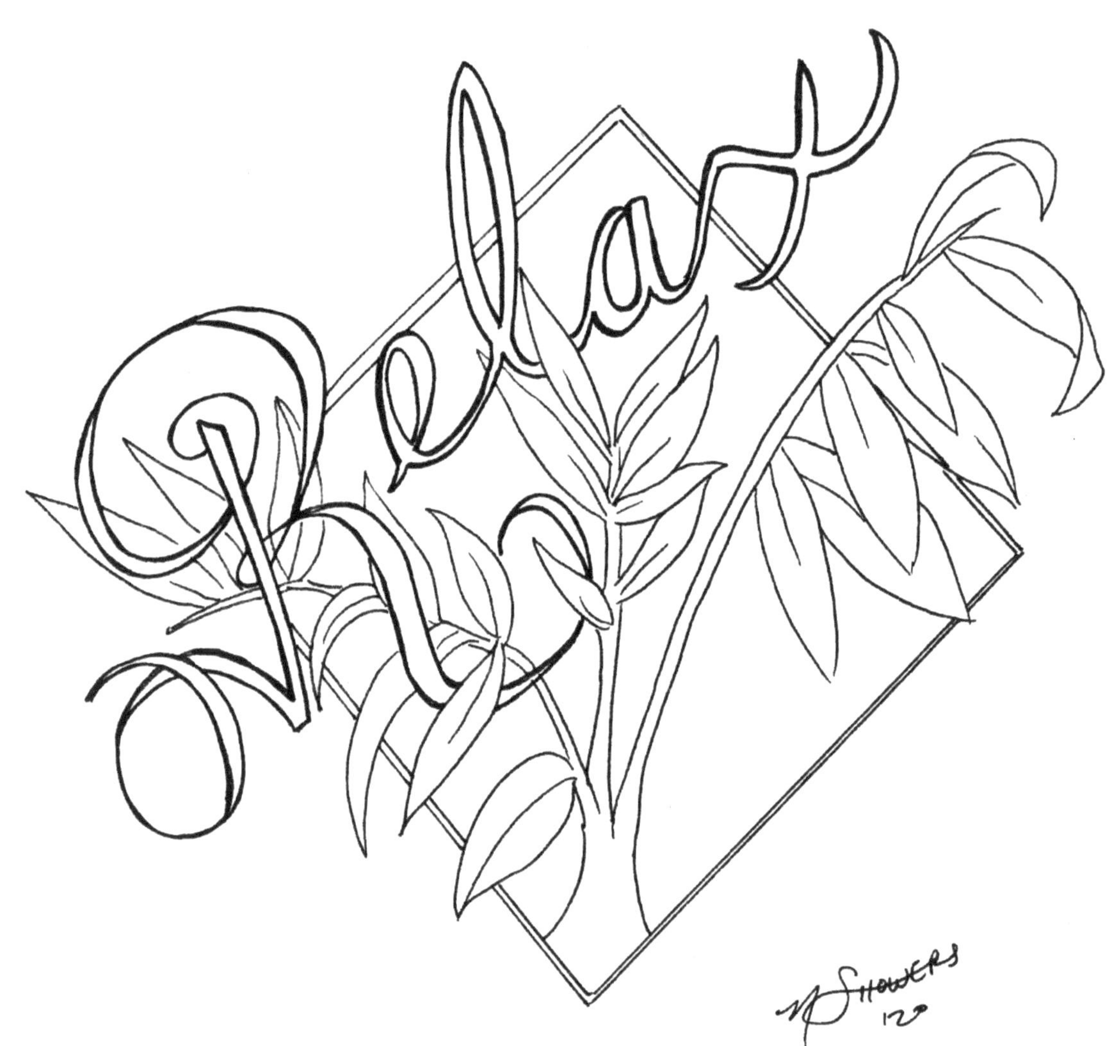
Relax

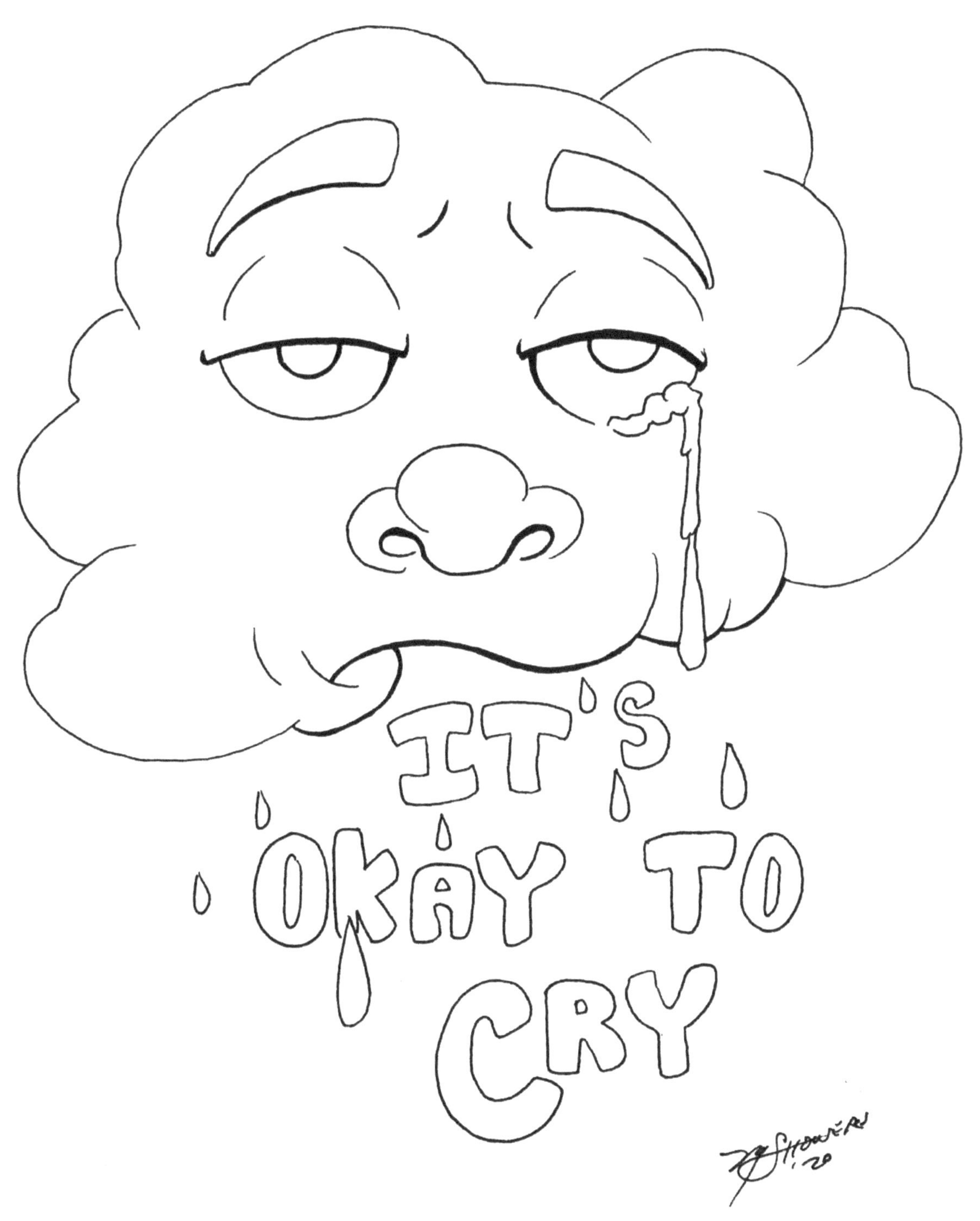
IT'S
OKAY TO
CRY

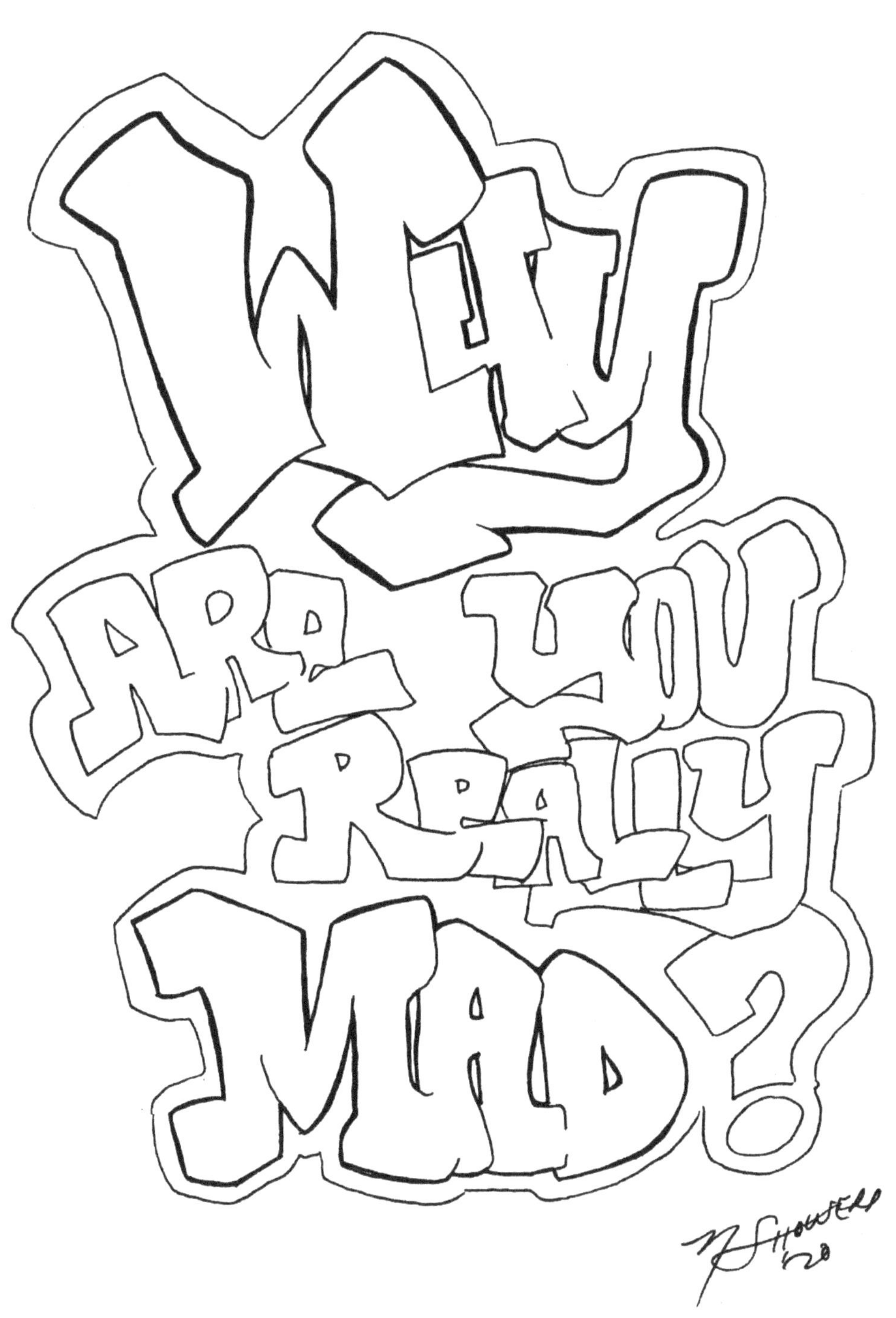
WHY
ARE YOU
REALLY
MAD?

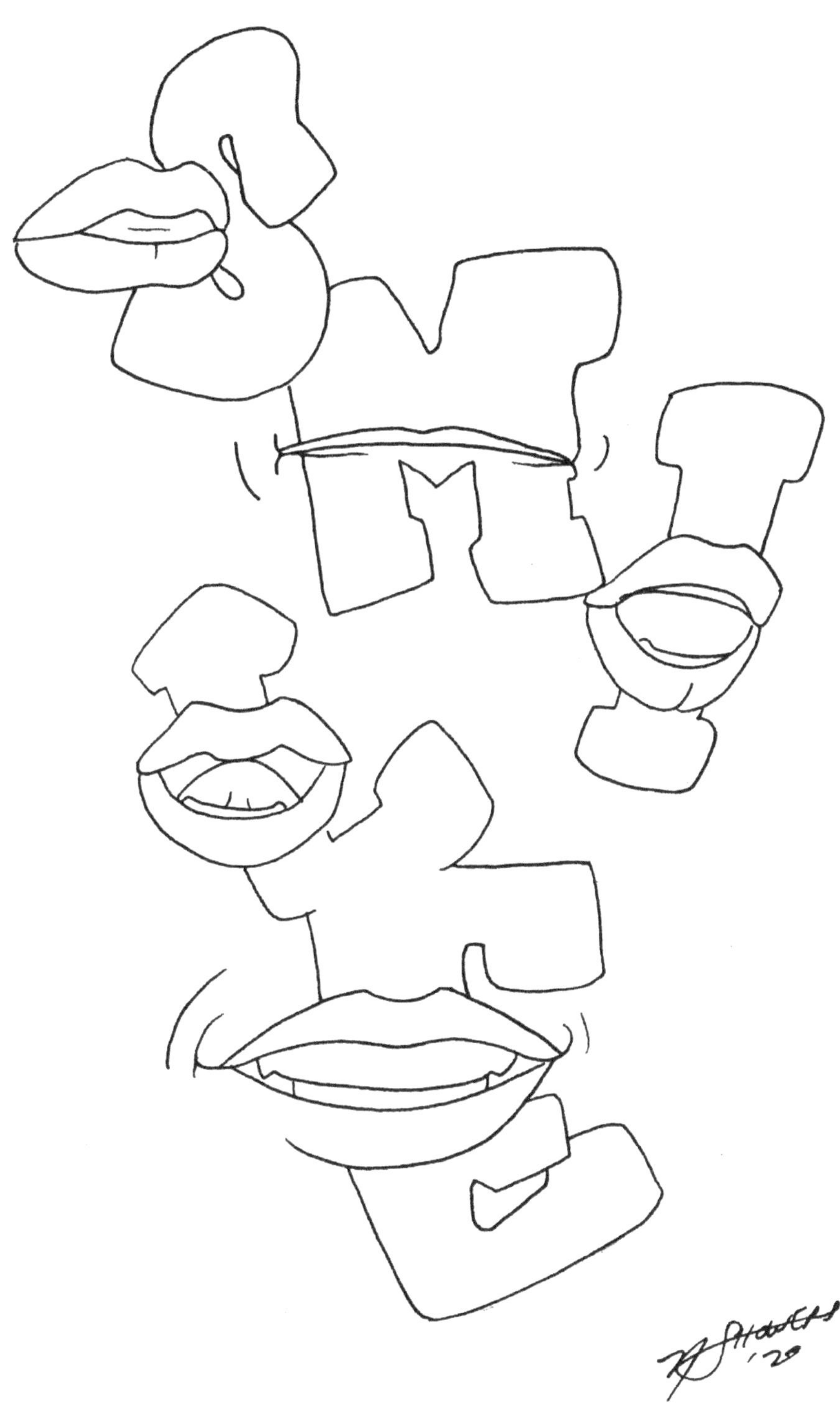

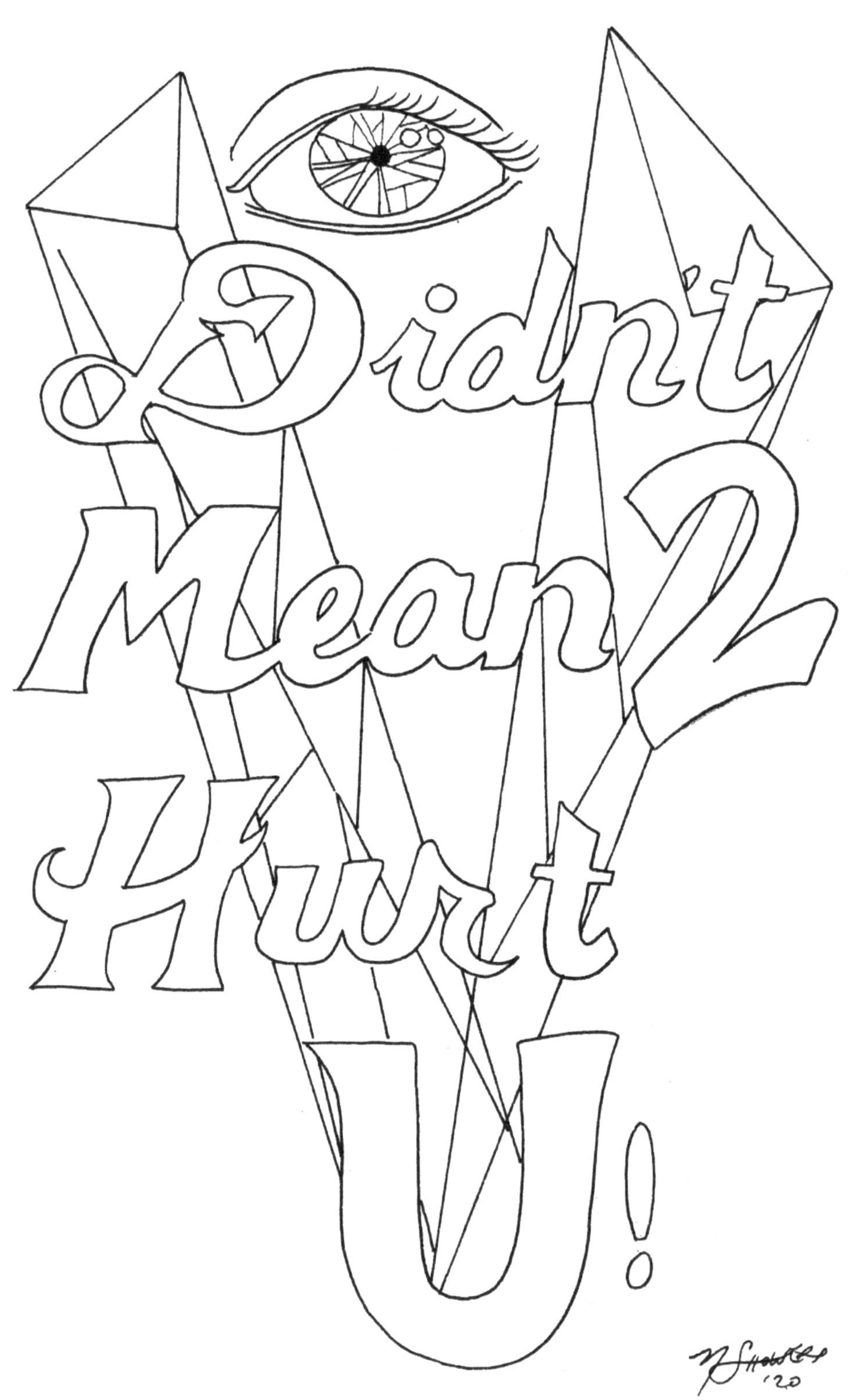
Didn't
Mean 2
Hurt
U!

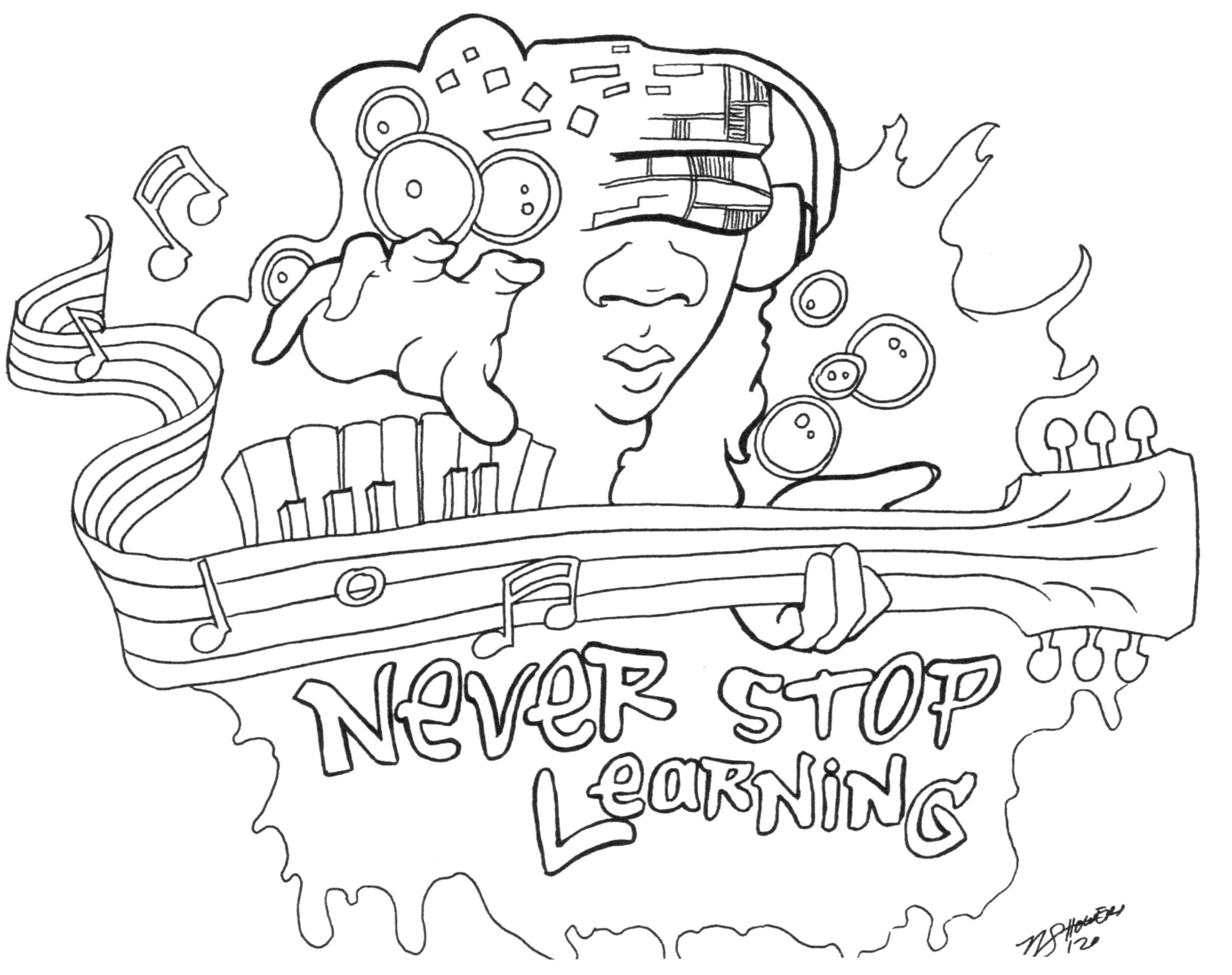
NEVER STOP
LEARNING

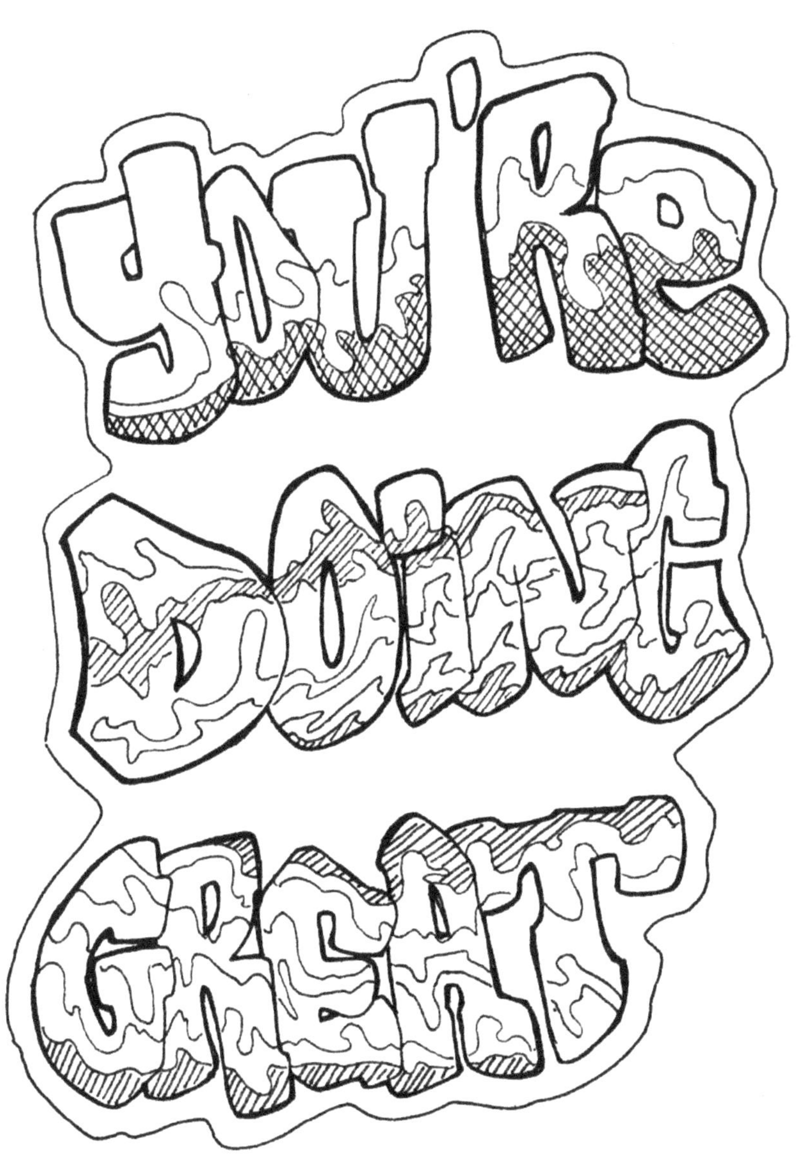
YOU'RE
DOING
GREAT

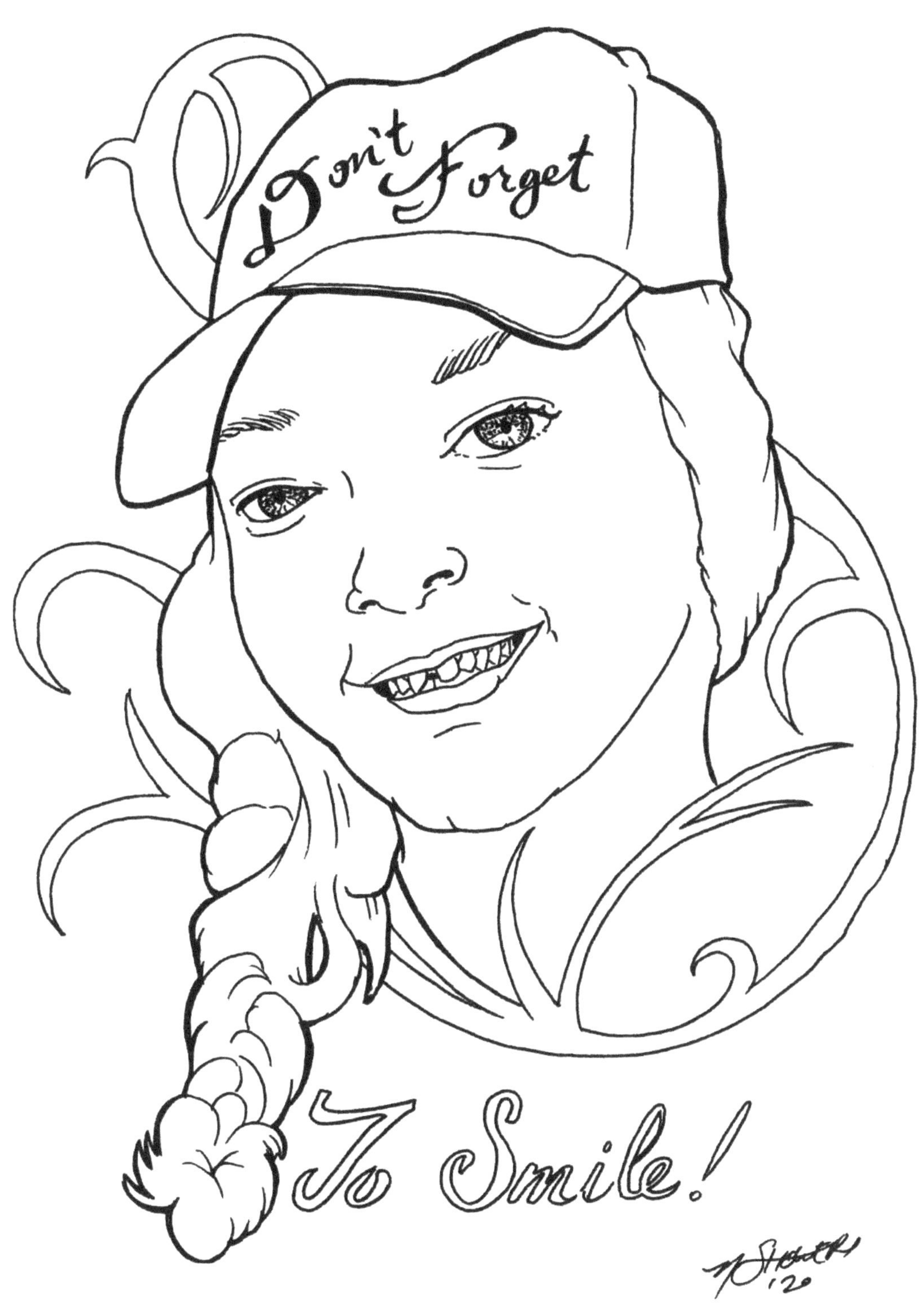
Don't Forget
To Smile!
'20

Advanced Designs

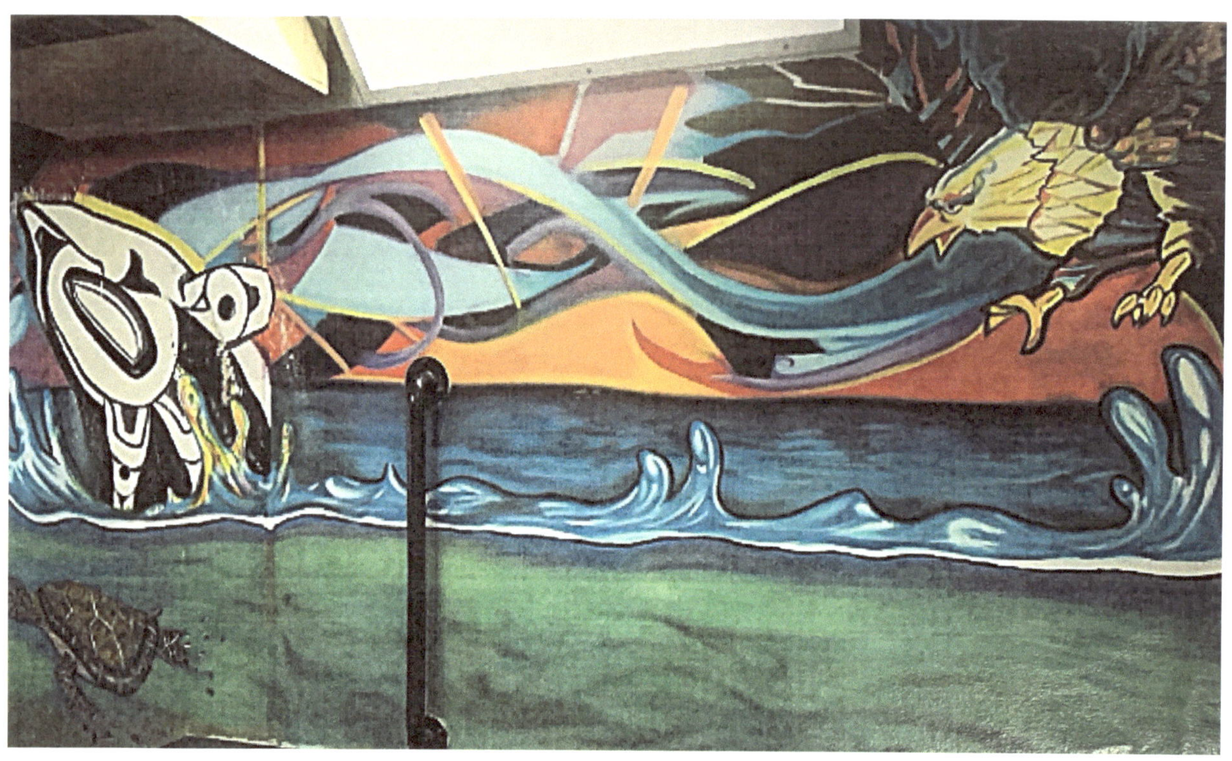

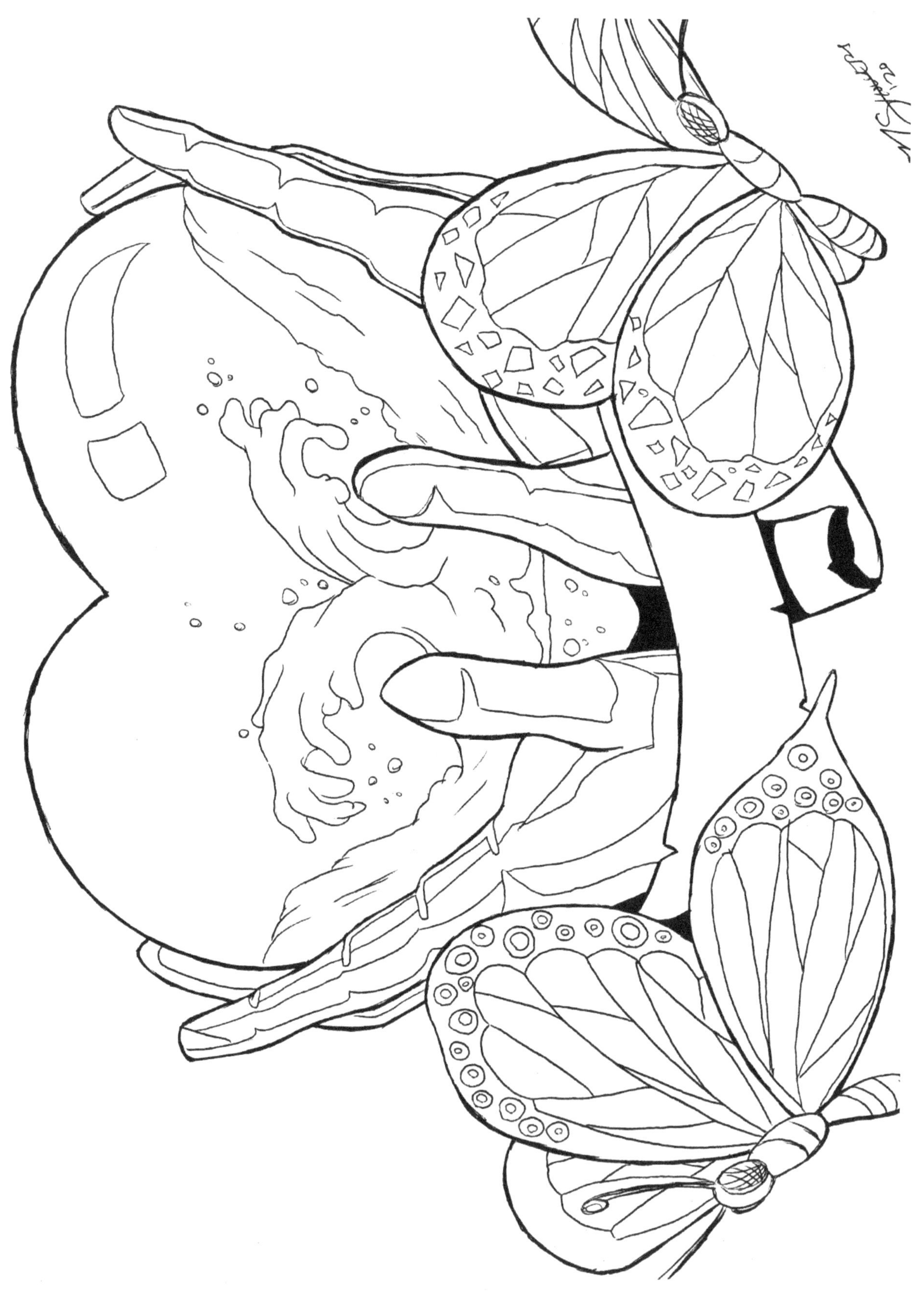

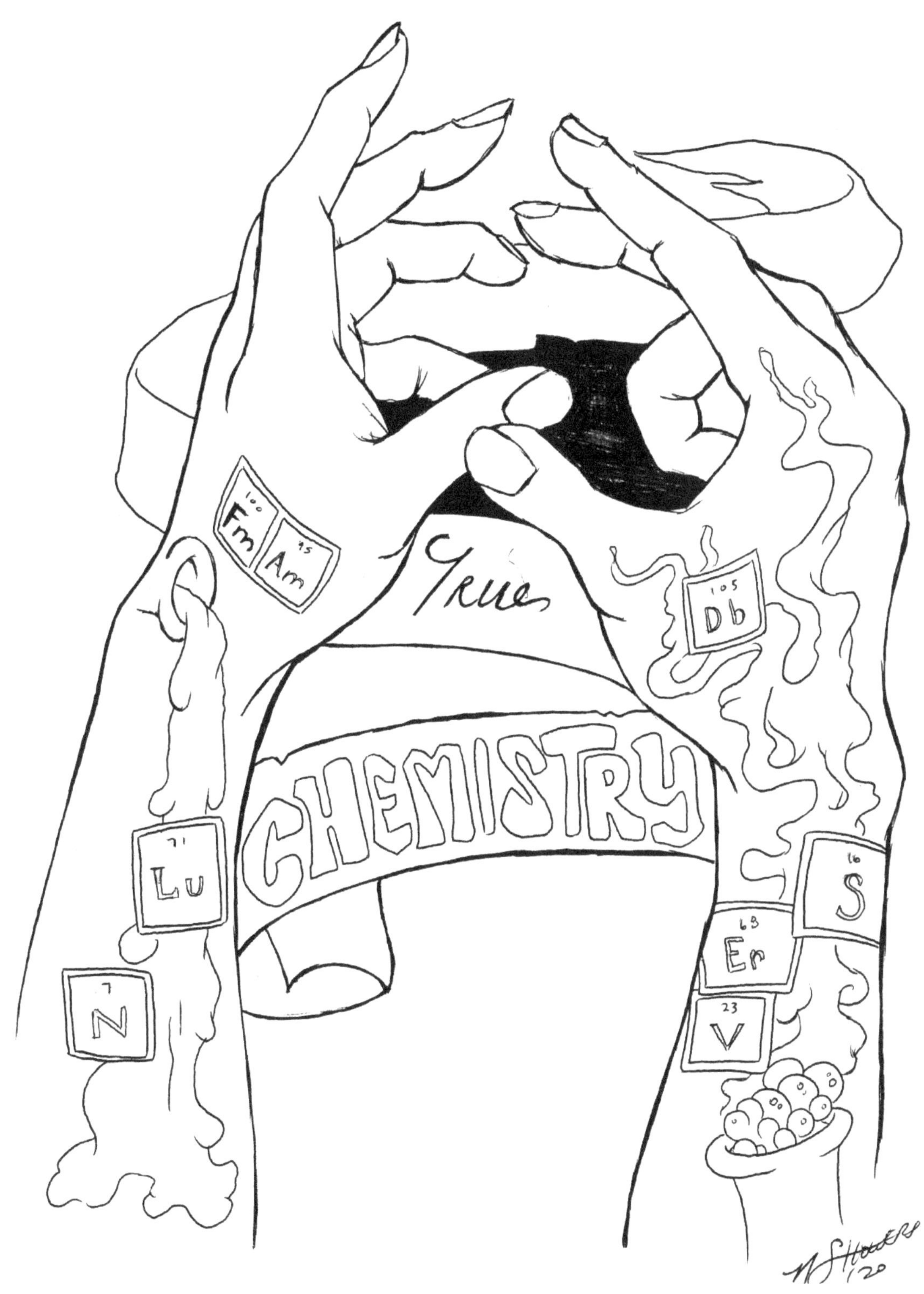

100 Fm
95 Am
True
105 Db
CHEMISTRY
71 Lu
7 N
16 S
68 Er
23 V

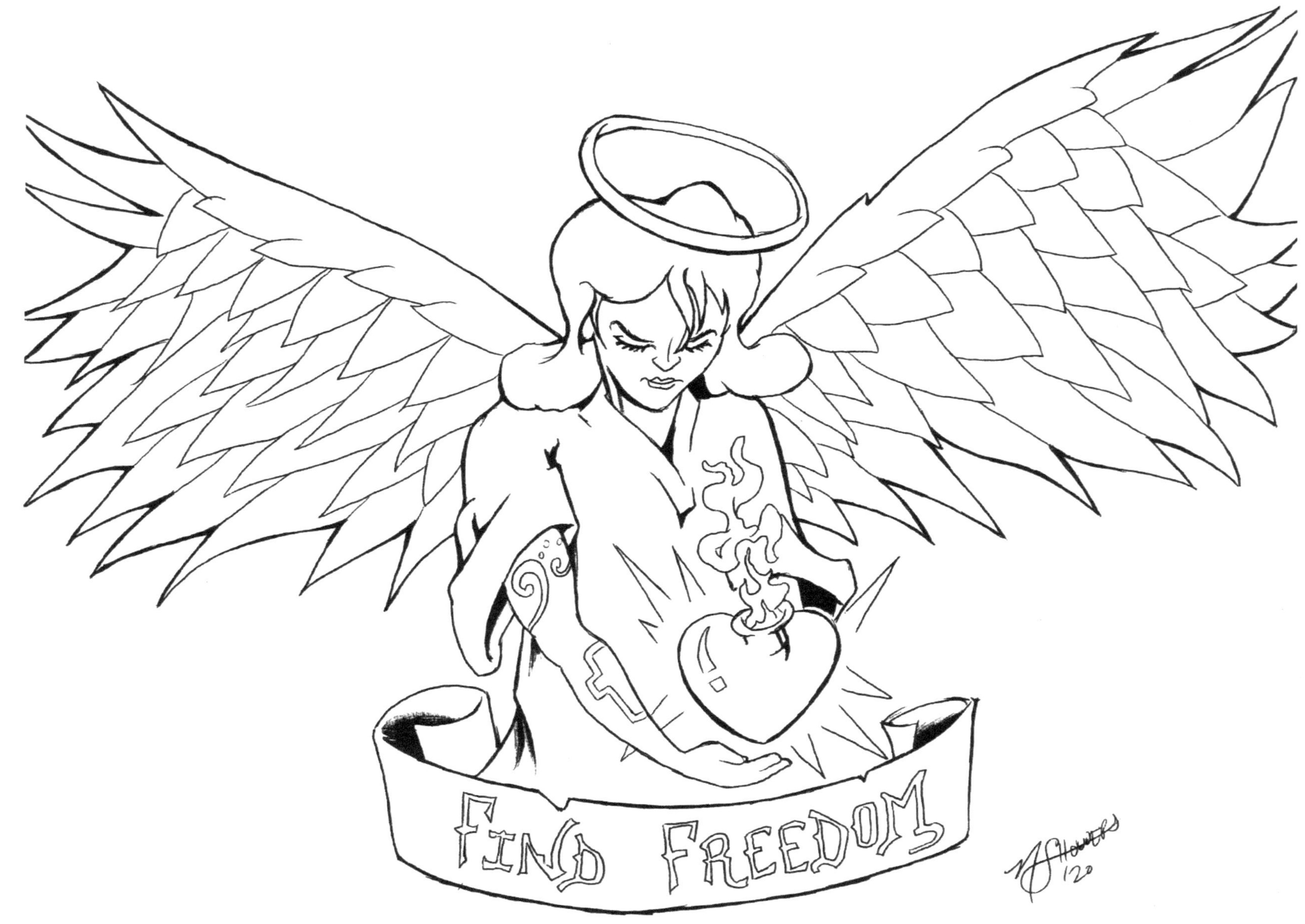
FIND FREEDOM

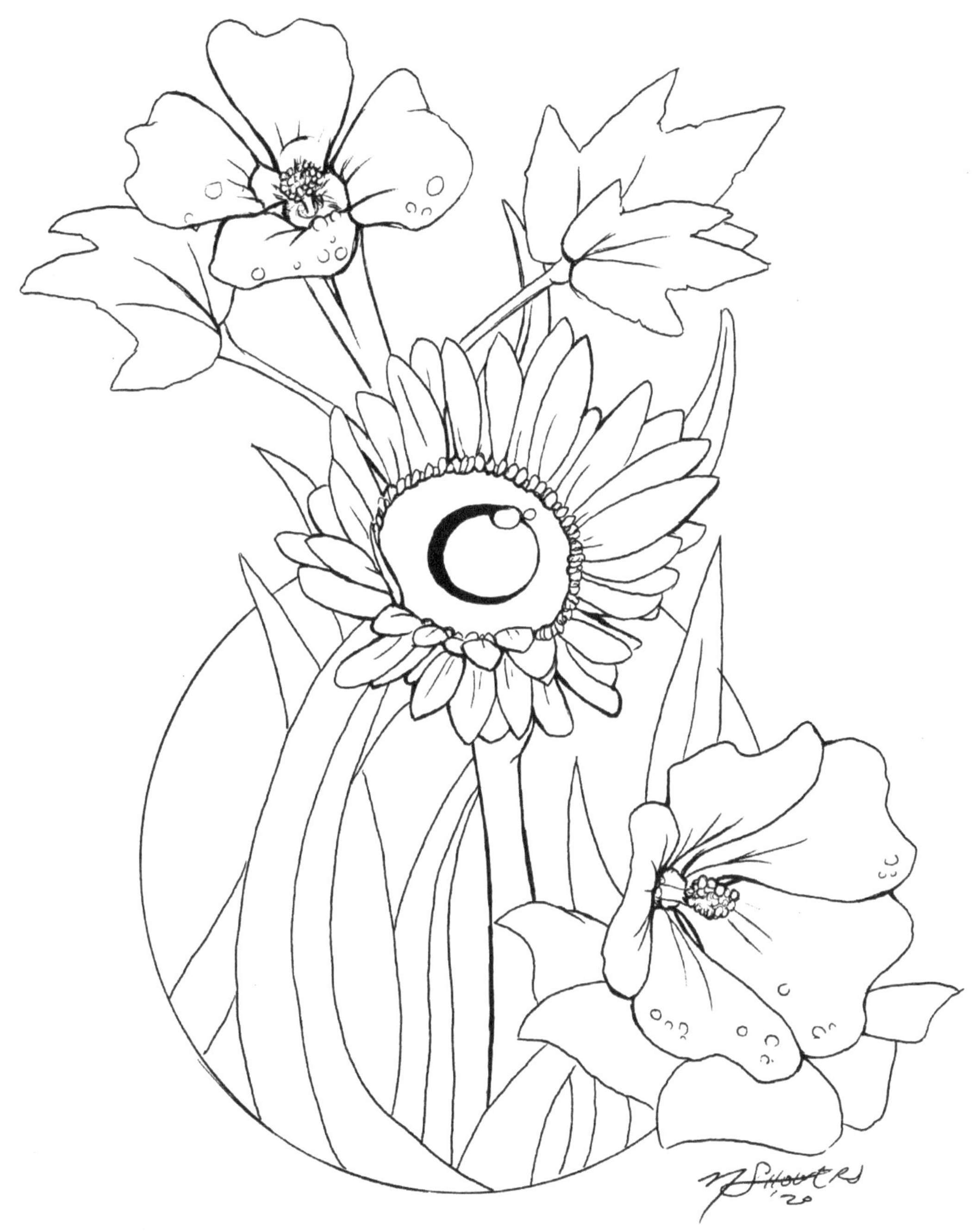

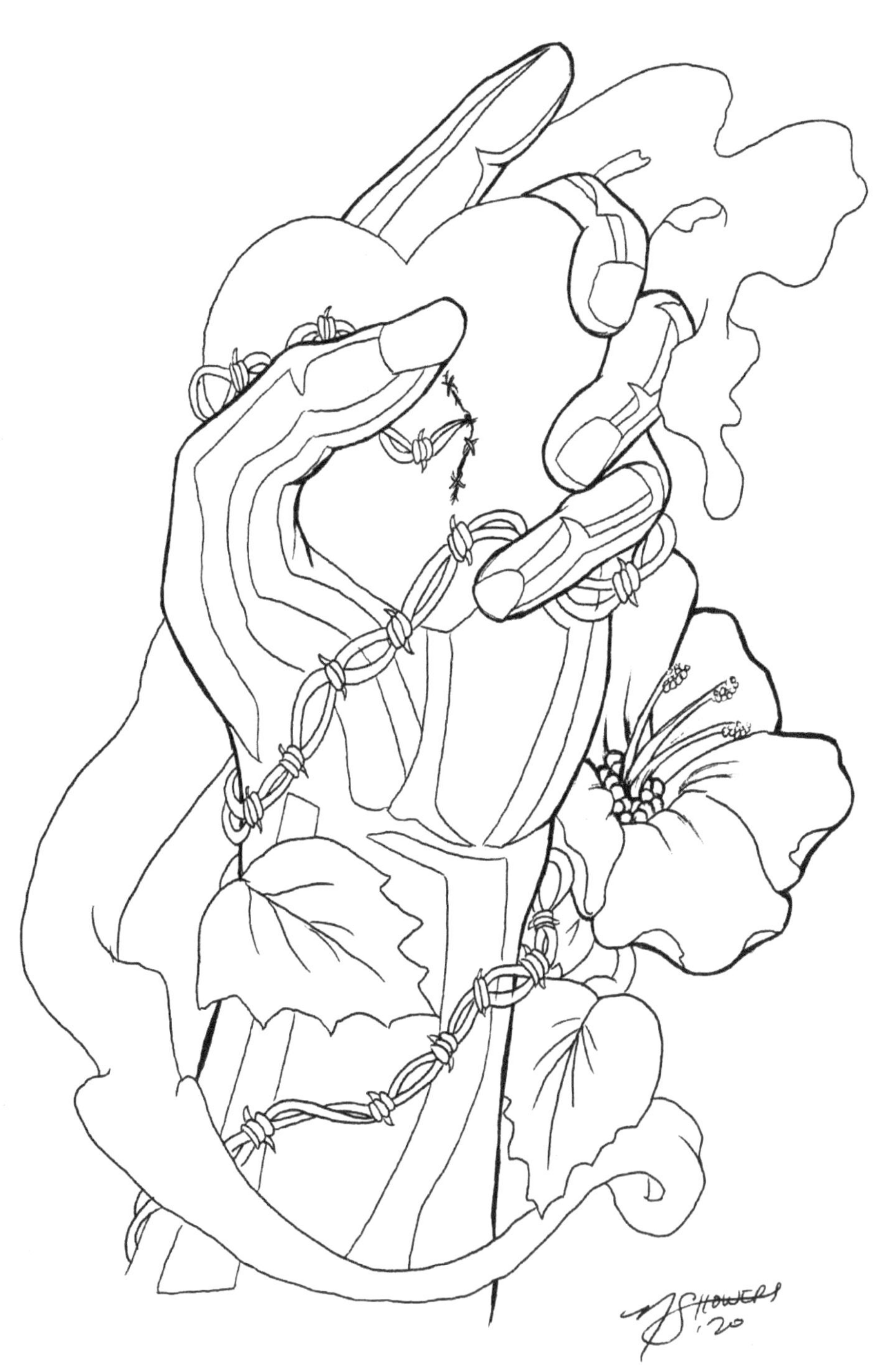
SHOWERS
'20

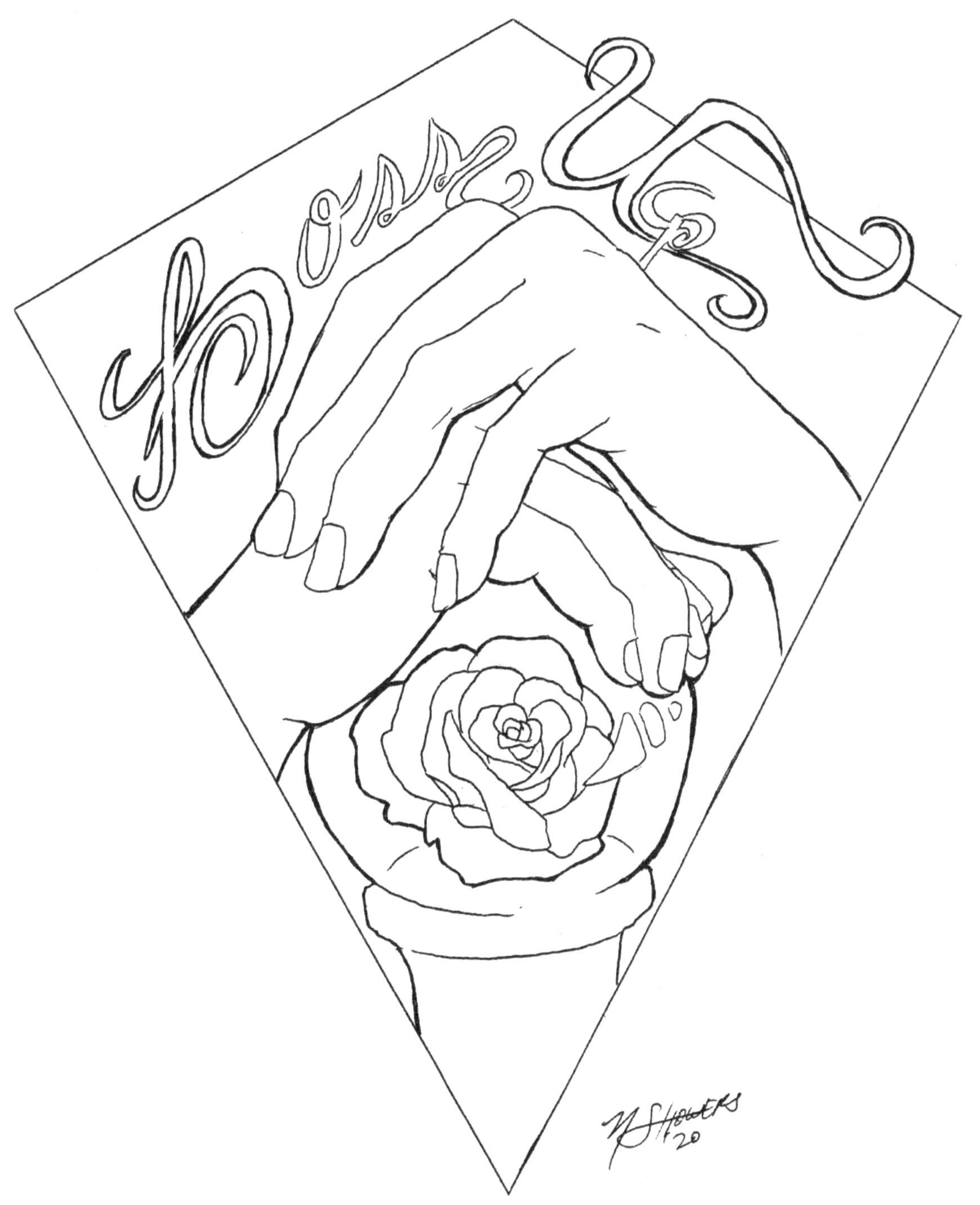
Boss Up

www.ingramcontent.com/pod-product-compliance
Lightning Source LLC
LaVergne TN
LVHW070153110826
845147LV00002B/389

* 9 7 8 0 5 7 8 7 7 3 1 8 6 *